TOUCHING THE UNSEEN WORLD

Other books by Betty Malz

My Glimpse of Eternity
Prayers that Are Answered
Super Natural Living
Angels Watching Over Me
Women in Tune
Heaven: A Bright and Shining Place

BETTY MALZ

TOUCHING THE UNSEEN WORLD

Published by

✓ chosen books

FLEMING H. REVELL COMPANY
TARRYTOWN, NEW YORK

Scripture quotations in this publication are from The New King James Version. Copyright © 1979, 1980, 1982 Thomas Nelson, Inc., Publishers.
Scripture quotations identified KJV are from the King James Version of the Bible.

Library of Congress Cataloging-in-Publication Data

Malz, Betty.
    Touching the unseen world / Betty Malz.
        p.   cm.
    ISBN 0-8007-9180-0 : $10.95
    1. Christian life—1960–   2. Miracles.   I. Title.
    BV4501.2.M336   1991
    231.7—dc20   91-10142
                                                                          CIP

A Chosen Book
Copyright © 1991 by Betty Malz

Chosen Books Publishing Company, Ltd.
Published by
Fleming H. Revell Company
Tarrytown, New York
Printed in the United States of America

This book is dedicated to my dad,
Glenn Perkins,
a real person
traveling to a real place!

Some things are neither here nor there,
some people are more here than there,
but he seems of late to be *more there than here!*

Dear Betty,

Let the world as well as the Church and heaven know without any doubt what you said about your account in heaven's bank being far greater than your earthly accounts all together, and that your treasure there is where your heart is also. I don't want anyone to be able to ask any questions about the sincerity of my Christianity and where my treasure is and why. Keep your eyes on the skies; you have much more there than your tithes.

Lots of love,
Dad

ACKNOWLEDGMENTS

Thanks to Len LeSourd who challenged me, "Perhaps the unseen world is the *real* world!" He worked long and hard through each rewrite, ironing out the wrinkles.

To Jane Campbell for this assignment and to Ann McMath for her editorial help. Thanks to them both for their friendship and for cheering me on during the setbacks.

To my daughter April who helped me with computer technique and ran errands, even though she was coaching basketball and attending college.

To Ed and Joyce Settle for hiding me in their "quiet place" during the rewrite.

To Mona Johnian for her research tape on heaven.

To Maria Foran for screening the phone calls.

To Helen Marquardt, the "anonymous investor."

To my brother Marvin Perkins . . . Uncle Earl Rodgers . . . Kevin Shorey . . . Jody Kay . . . and Paul and Tracy Hamelink for stories, quotes and exhortations and Ed and Ruth Schlossmacher for Scripture help.

To Amy Emery, Ruth Danyo and Pearl Wiseman who supplied

me with fruit and snacks that provided energy during the long hours
of typing.

To Tissy's Boutique for my costume.

To my photographer/husband, Carl Malz.

To my hair stylist, Jack Cocilova.

CONTENTS

PREFACE

The invisible world is the real world, for it is our forever and permanent home! God had the universal plan of eternity well in mind before the foundations of the earth we know were ever laid.

As part of that plan, you were "in the heart of God" before the foundation of the world. You were conceived by the act of His divine love and can share in the bloodline of Jesus' sacrifice, through the direct lineage of His mercy.

The earth is the "womb." We are in this womb being formed, developed and soon to be delivered that we might inherit the heavenly Kingdom. There we will dwell, even reign with Him around His eternal throne in the Forever Land. "It has not yet been revealed what we shall be, but we know that when He is revealed, we shall be like Him, for we shall see Him as He is" (1 John 3:2).

There may or may not be life on other planets, but of one thing we can be sure: God cared deeply for the earth. Of all the planets out in space, He chose for His only Son to be born, to live and to die here. "The Word became flesh and dwelt among us" (John 1:14). He sent His Son from heaven and built a bridge from there to here. He chose a virgin on earth to bear His Son, conceived by the Holy Ghost. The virgin Mary didn't get to name her baby, but what a name God gave Him—a name above every name, above all principalities and powers both in heaven and in the earth!

It may seem that the idea of an invisible world is incompatible with the discoveries science has made about our universe. That is probably because an unseen world does not seem very scientific. God is, however, infinitely involved in the science of the universe. God is omniscient. Taken from two words—*omni* meaning "infinite" and *scientia* meaning science—His omniscience means that God is the infinite, all-knowing Scientist.

As Dr. Wernher von Braun once said, "Science and religion are sisters. Science strives to know more about creation while Christians try better to understand the Creator."

My brother Marvin Perkins helped build the electronics used to monitor the Apollo 8 flight that went around the moon in 1968. When Frank Borman returned from that mission he was met by a straightforward reporter who asked him this question: "A Soviet cosmonaut returned from a space flight recently and commented that he saw neither God nor angels on his flight. Did you see God up there?"

Frank Borman replied, "No, I did not see Him, but I saw His evidence everywhere."

In this book we, too, will be looking at the evidence. His unseen world is everywhere apparent—if you know how to look. You will discover that you actually have access to the creative power of the unseen world. King David, the psalmist, learned that his help came from the Lord who made the heavens and the earth. The Lord is the Source. He has created and will supply your needs. You will never be the same once you learn how to reach out and touch the unseen world . . . once it touches you.

Does this sound too good to be true? Then think of this. Have you ever noticed that the more you pray, the more coincidences happen? I have. And the converse, the less I pray the fewer coincidences I experience.

Here is one example fresh in my mind. I do not believe it to be a mere coincidence that I should be writing of angelic intervention and the return of Jesus from the unseen world for this book during the week of Christmas. There is an old English legend that says just as angels hovered over the earth when Christ was born, so they linger near the earth during the season in which we celebrate His birth. And I have heard a number of Bible prophets who believe that since we celebrate His coming during the Church season of Advent, Jesus will come again to receive us to Himself and take us from this world at Christmastime.

Maybe so. There is certainly much that we will not know until we live and reign with Jesus in that as yet unseen world. And I feel quite sure that when that happens, we will look back to our lives in this world with much amusement. Our philosophy too often is "I'll believe it when I see it." Well, we are in for great surprises!

Yet even though we are limited by space and time and dimension in this life, God has given us wonderful wisps of insight into that other world—things we can "touch," if we reach out in faith.

That is the purpose of this book. We will explore the ways God joyously shares the world to come with us here and now. We long for our eternal home; in fact, those of us who have received Jesus Christ as Savior have begun to live in eternity already. We have great help and protection and insight available to us simply because He loves us and wants us to know about that great love.

Walk with me through the following chapters as we see all that God has shown us about His invisible world and find ways to tap heaven's resources. "The things which are seen are temporary, but the things which are not seen are eternal" (2 Corinthians 4:18). These are the things that count.

1

WHEN THE UNSEEN WORLD TOUCHES YOU

When the unseen world touches you, you will experience supernatural joy, the reality of God, living in the very marrow of your bones! It is joy inexpressible and full of glory (1 Peter 1:8). It is unmerited, cannot be earned, but a good and perfect gift sent down from God above by mercy and grace. The miraculous power of the unseen world is reachable; the invisible is accessible; it will be accompanied by a peace that passes all understanding and comprehension.

Have you desired this touch? Perhaps you have wondered if it is even possible. Let me assure you:

If your heart is reaching, all heaven will help you. To illustrate this mystery, I offer these six ways in which a person may be touched, reached by the power of the invisible world: Jesus Himself may appear; a blinding light from heaven may shine (as with Saul); a supernatural voice may speak from within; angels may visit; supernatural wisdom may come through another human being; or a miraculous answer to prayer may be given.

Why does God reach down and touch some people and not others? I believe God knows the heart that is searching and reaching for Him. He knows the end from the beginning, reads our genuine motives, and in His overruling, practical providence realizes what that person would do with His power once it became available.

Let's look at each of the six ways we may be touched by the unseen world.

Jesus Himself Appears

We were living in South Dakota several years ago when I got a phone call from a Catholic sister, Ann, who worked in a children's hospital about 31 miles from our home. She invited me to come and meet the parents of a young patient she had been attending who had just had a very curious and mysterious experience. Having read my book *My Glimpse of Eternity*, she felt that I could help the little fellow's parents understand what had happened to their son.

When I arrived, I heard the story. Little Tommie was only two years old. His mother, a Catholic, and his father, a Protestant, decided when they were married that, because of family conflicts, neither of them would ever mention God or attend any church.

At two, Tommie contracted pneumonia. When his parents realized he could not breathe properly, they called an ambulance. The paramedics arrived, noted his bluish color and tried to administer oxygen. Just before reaching the hospital, Tommie quit responding.

In the emergency room, the attending physician performed a tracheotomy. Tommie's vital signs were gone and they pronounced him dead. Four minutes later the nurse, Sister Ann, noticed that Tommie's lips were moving. When he opened his eyes the family was shocked, yet Tommie's response was not fear, but pure excitement! The nurse placed her finger over the windpipe to enable him to speak.

Looking directly at his daddy, he said, "Jesus loves me!"

His dad suspected that one of the Catholic sisters had said something to the child, for he asked the boy quickly, "Who told you that?"

Tommie answered, *"He* told me. I saw Him.*"*
The invisible world had touched that little fellow. As I talked with his parents, I marveled at what loving mercy God has shown us in these glimpses of Himself in a world we are hesitant to believe in.

A Blinding Light from Heaven

Not all impressions of the unseen world are given in the quietness of our hearts. The invisible world touched Saul in a mighty, dramatic way. Saul, a highly educated man, was affiliated with the Sanhedrin court. He was perhaps a practicing attorney, briefcase in hand, about his work of imprisoning Christians. Acts 9:1 says he breathed out threats and murder against the disciples of the Lord.

Suddenly as he walked along the road toward Damascus, a dazzling light straight down from the unseen world shone around him and he fell to the ground. He heard an audible voice from the unseen source of the light saying, "Saul, why are you persecuting Me?" Saul asked, "Who are You, Lord?" (I believe that when the unseen world touches you, you already know.)

"I am Jesus, whom you are persecuting."

Trembling, Saul asked, "Lord, what do You want me to do?" He was instructed to go into the city. If Saul had been traveling alone, we might reason that he had suffered a sunstroke, but verse 7 tells us that the men traveling with him were speechless, hearing the voice, too, but seeing no one. (They all heard from the invisible world.) Saul was instantly blind and so utterly preoccupied that he did not eat or even sip water for three days.

In the city of Damascus was a godly man named Ananias who had a vision in which he saw the Lord and heard His voice from the unseen world telling him to go to Saul. At first Ananias hesitated because of Saul's reputation, but the Lord assured him that He had prearranged the visit. (God will never tell you to do anything that He has not first ordained, organized and fully equipped you to do.)

Ananias went, following instructions. Saul's eyes were opened, he received the Holy Spirit and became perhaps the greatest evangelist the world has known.

What a turnaround for Saul!

That was no ordinary voice he heard, from no ordinary place. God from heaven had spoken. And as the directives Saul was given bore fruit, he could exclaim, "I was not disobedient to the heavenly vision." (Time will always tell when any revelation is of God above.) he the persecutor now became Paul the missionary, traveling and proclaiming the good news of the eternal Kingdom to come. He says of himself in 1 Timothy 1:13: "I was formerly a blasphemer, a persecutor, and an insolent man; but I obtained mercy because I did it ignorantly in unbelief."

The whole theme of the first two chapters of Ephesians is that God's grace abounded toward us, forgiving our sins, giving us wisdom and prudence, making known to us the mystery of His will, according to His good pleasure. He was looking for us long before we were looking for Him, making it possible for us to sit together in heavenly places. He knew us so we could know Him and the riches of His glory. He is even now looking down upon you, while you read, while you wonder, while you are searching and reasoning. You are Jesus' reward for Calvary! He has wanted you from the foundation of the world.

A Supernatural Voice from Within

The invisible world may reach us by a knowing, a prompting, an echo of the heart—our "inner voice." This happened to a young medical doctor friend of mine just recently. I tell the story here with his permission, but have changed the names to protect the family's privacy.

Dr. Eric Van, his wife, Pamela, and four small sons were enjoying a vacation trip in their van when—whoom!—grief struck. It had been a very hot day, and now it was raining, so they had bedded down the four boys in the back of the van to sleep while Dr. Van and his wife drove during the cool night hours. The young couple seldom enjoyed uninterrupted quiet time together with four active little boys. The oldest, Terry, had just turned nine and had talked of little else but swimming at the resort the next day.

Reaching for a Coke from the cooler on the floor of the van, Dr. Van accidentally bumped the steering wheel and sent the vehicle careening into the path of a moving van. The sound of the impact was deafening!

When they finally stopped spinning from the impact, Eric and Pamela crawled from the wreckage, stunned and bleeding, to find that the large truck had severed their vehicle in two, and the back half, containing the four sleeping boys, was gone! Stumbling through the dark, rainy night toward the sound of the boys' fearful screams, Dr. Van stumbled against a small body that had been thrown against a fence. It was Terry.

He told Carl and me: "I dropped down beside him, sobbing, listening for any sound of heartbeat. He was dead. Grief overwhelmed me, paralyzed my thinking. My energy even to move from that spot deadened within me. I knew at that point that I would never leave that ditch along the roadside and go on living."

He heard his wife calling. In the darkness, she had finally found the other three boys. They were hurt badly, but alive. Suddenly the doctor heard another voice, louder than his wife's, though it did not speak audibly. *Go on to the living,* thundered the "voice" inside his spirit.

Suddenly he looked up and saw a yellow spotlight. It seemed to be coming from a different world, and even though he was still crouched over the body of his son, he saw Terry running in the warmth of that light through a grassy meadow. Laughing voices of other children rang out. Perfect specimens of animals scurried to let him run past, and he plunged happily down a green velvet bank and into the river below. He joined the other children—splashing, playing, laughing as they swam together in a river where they could never drown. The water was crystal clear. It was, Dr. Van knew, the river of life.

Go on to the living, the inner voice echoed, as if amplified from that other shore. The doctor removed his coat, wrapped his son's body in it and joined his wife and other children. A passerby had already called an ambulance, which arrived shortly. The family was hospitalized for several days. Two of the boys suffered serious injuries that required therapy for weeks.

It has been six months now, and Dr. Van still cannot explain how it happened, but he was healed on the spot of grief. It was not natural; it was supernatural. That inner voice and vision of the unseen world where Terry is has given him peace. Since Terry's transfer to that world, the family feels linked to eternity. They have an anchor holding them to the invisible world. That loving pull will draw them someday for a family reunion to where Terry is already.

How many times, if we listen, might that inner voice comfort or guide us as well?

Angels May Visit

Angels from the invisible world can touch us, anytime, anywhere.

Whenever something is mentioned for the first time in Scripture, we should pay close attention. Let's consider the first time that an angel ever came down to the earth. It was not at Jesus' birth, our Christmas celebration, but the very first time an angel appeared on this earth was to Hagar and her son in the wilderness where they had fled for their lives, and were now dying.

God had promised Abraham that Sarah would bear him a son and that seed would become as numerous as the sands of the sea, a mighty nation. When it did not happen after a certain number of years, Sarah suggested that Abram take Hagar, her personal maid, and produce his son by her.

Hagar became the pawn in a huge game of outstepping God's timing. It may have looked enticing for Abraham, an old man, to make love to a young woman. He did, and she conceived. Sarah, forgetting that it was her own idea, became very jealous of both Hagar and the baby boy, Ishmael.

Soon after, Sarah conceived and bore Abraham's promised child, Isaac. Abraham loved Hagar's child as well as Sarah's, but to bring peace, he sent her and Ishmael away. When they were hungry in that wilderness, and dying of thirst, the child prayed. God heard him, and the angel of God called to Hagar out of heaven: "What ails you, Hagar? Fear not, for God has heard the voice of the lad where he is. Arise, lift up the lad and hold him with your hand, for I will make him a great nation" (Genesis 21:17–18).

God opened Hagar's eyes and she saw a supernatural well of water; and she went and filled the bottle with water and gave the boy a drink.

Ishmael lived and grew and did indeed become the father of a mighty nation—the Arab world.

Angels are an important and fascinating link with the unseen world, and we learn from this story that they are accurate messengers, relaying God's purposes to His people.

Supernatural Wisdom through Another Human Being

The unseen world touches us sometimes through the wisdom of other human beings and, in a very practical way, meets a private but desperate need.

Nick grew up in eastern Illinois with several brothers. They enjoyed playing in the deep water in a gravel pit near their home. One Memorial Day at a family picnic when Nick was eight, one of his brothers shoved him off his inner tube and sent him sprawling into the water. He panicked and, had his father not jumped in and rescued him, would surely have drowned. The boy developed a paralyzing fear of water.

Nick married and moved to Florida, but he never enjoyed living here because of his horrible fear of water. His young son loved the water and begged for a boat, but Nick would not even drive over the famous Sunshine Skyway bridge that spans the Gulf between St. Petersburg and Sarasota, much less get into a boat. He eventually moved his family back to Illinois, simply to escape the constant presence of water in the Sunshine State.

One day Nick felt comfortable enough to share his fear with a friend. After much discussion, his friend said, "Nick, come out in my boat with me and I'll prove to you how unfounded those childhood fears really are. You are robbing yourself and your family of pleasure. I'm not asking you to walk on the water like Peter in the Bible. I'll put two life jackets on you. I will put you between myself and another close friend who is a strong swimmer, and we'll conquer this invisible foe once and for all." Nick consented.

The scheduled day was the longest day of his life. All morning he dreaded the two o'clock boating date with those two men. Finally it was time to climb into the boat. It was his first time in the water in 26 years and he felt panic. They were out on the water for only a few minutes when an oncoming boat equipped with a 76-h.p. Evinrude swept by and their boat began to rock. Three minutes later, Nick opened his eyes slowly. He was alive! He did not drown in those mini-waves. Later, wearing a life preserver, he let the two men slip him down into the water and prove that he could float. After that day he went to the Y.M.C.A. and learned to swim properly.

Shortly after this recovery, he shared his two favorite Scriptures with me, which he calls the "swimmer's special friends." They are: "When you pass through the waters, I will be with you; and through the rivers, they shall not overflow you" (Isaiah 43:2) and "Fear not, for I am with you; be not dismayed, for I am your God. I will strengthen you, yes, I will help you, I will uphold you with My righteous right hand" (Isaiah 41:10).

A Miraculous Answer to Prayer

Witnessing a miracle in an impossible situation is another way the invisible world serves us, through our faith and prayers.

My friend Barbara Johnson lives in La Habra, California. You may have read her books telling of the devastating years her family suffered, stories told with warmth and an amazing gentle humor in spite of the pain. Her husband spent two years in the hospital following a severe automobile accident. One of her three sons was killed in Vietnam, another died in a car crash and the third, Larry, confessed that he was homosexual, left the family and changed his name. Barbara spent eleven years wondering if he was dead or alive.

Last year when her doctor told her she had diabetes she couldn't even worry, so paralyzed with disappointment was she already on a long-term basis.

Barbara told me: "When anxiety closed in, my best move was to turn to the Lord for His invisible help from heaven. I took a grip with my tired hands, stood firm on my shaky legs and Hebrews 12:12: 'Strengthen the hands which hang down, and the feeble knees; and make straight paths for your feet, so that what is lame may . . . be healed.' "

In spite of her circumstances, she was amazed to find she could laugh again. The Lord's joy kept the stress under control and accelerated the healing of her tortured, fractured mind.

She hung onto hope from on high and His Word: "I will . . . [make] the Valley of Achor [troubles] as a door of hope" (Hosea 2:15).

Last Mother's Day her son Larry appeared at her door. "I have a Mother's Day gift for you," he said, though he held out no package. After hugs and tears of joy to see him again, she found out what it was. "I went to an old-fashioned Holy Ghost meeting," he said. "I received prayer and I want you to know that I have been cleansed, delivered from the deception and perversion of homosexuality." (This was his gift to her, an invisible gift from the invisible Kingdom.)

In her book *Stick a Geranium in Your Hat and Be Happy,* she wrote of this experience and concluded, "I'm glad I stormed heaven's gate. The Lord has opened His floodgates of joy. The world to come touched us! My husband and I were trapped in an eleven-year parenthesis of pain. Then God kicked the end out of our parenthesis and our family was set free!''

There is no sorrow in that forever place, and the Johnson family has gotten a foretaste of it here. Larry is working with his parents in their "Spatula Ministry," helping others learn to cope with the pain of having a loved one trapped in homosexual behavior. Their theme song has become "Heaven Came Down and Glory Filled My Soul.''

Three times in history the Persons of the Godhead have touched our planet earth. First, God made a mini-heaven in the form of the Garden of Eden to show us what the invisible world, His place, was like. Then He came down and walked and talked with Adam and Eve.

The second visit from the unseen world was when Jesus left the golden throne of the celestial city, where He was reigning with God, His Father, was born as a baby to the virgin Mary, lived with us and died for us to make a way for us to live with Him throughout eternity.

The third visit was from the Holy Spirit, after Jesus ascended back to the Father and sent the eternal Comforter to abide with us, in us.

The unseen world will touch each of us one more time, either through our personal death (as 2 Corinthians 5:8 says, to be absent from the body is to be present with the Lord), or through corporate rapture to take us to Himself in the invisible Kingdom forever (quoting 1 Thessalonians 4:16: "For the Lord Himself will descend from heaven with a shout, with the voice of an archangel, and with the trumpet of God. And the dead in Christ will rise first. Then we who are alive and remain shall be caught up together with them. . . . And thus we shall always be with the Lord''").

We must keep aloof from all that is perishable and cling to only the eternal and the absolute. We have access to the heavenlies with Jesus as our advocate. When we pray to God through Jesus, He grants our petitions—for redemption from sin, healing from sickness and fortification with supernatural strength and power of the Holy Spirit.

You cannot touch the unseen world by faith until first the unseen world touches you (chooses you). "I will pour out My Spirit on all flesh; . . . I will show wonders in the heavens and in the earth. . . . And it shall come to pass that whoever calls on the name of the Lord shall be saved" (Joel 2:28, 30, 32).

God makes the first move toward us, then we respond. Every person is born with a conscience. As we mature, I believe opportunity comes to everyone either to reject or accept Jesus as Lord. I believe that God taps each human being on the shoulder, gives at least once in a lifetime the opportunity to accept or reject a passport to eternity, through Jesus. He is not willing that any should perish but that *all* should come to repentance.

When you pray that initial prayer, "Lord, be merciful to me a sinner," He hears every prayer that you pray thereafter.

Whoever will may come and take of the waters of life freely. When God moves toward us, we respond. "God demonstrates His own love toward us, in that while we were still sinners, Christ died for us" (Romans 5:8). This is the "prevenient grace" that John Wesley spoke of, the merciful grace of God that comes to us. He existed from the foundation of the world. He made this world for us; He made us for Himself. The first step was God's; He touched us. We reach out to Him and we desire Him even as we are His desire! Because of Jesus, fallen mankind is redeemed and can go back with Him to that perfect, permanent world.

In the course of this book we will explore the unseen world the power and protection afforded there as well as links connecting us and why Satan tries to hinder us from discovering it.

Come with me and discover how much there is to see in the unseen world.

2
INVISIBLE ENERGY

*I*nvisible does not mean nonexistent. I am amazed at the unexplainables that we enjoy. Who can deny the force of electricity? Each time I fly in a jet plane I ask, "How does it work, really?" Nobody has seen a headache or met depression and we don't know the color of pain. Then there's the "energy crisis." You cannot see energy. We take vitamins to stimulate our energy, yet what is it that gives us vitality?

We understand how necessary it is to do our "homework"—eat properly, rest properly and exercise daily to ensure our natural physical resources. But when stress and outside pressure depress us, when burnout and fatigue bankrupt us, can we have access to the supernatural Source? Will the creative power of the Holy Ghost fill us? I believe so.

I think that any believing child of God can walk into heaven's savings and loan company and tap into the Source of needed resources here on earth. The president and founding father of the Bank of Heaven is still in charge there.

I do my banking at a small green building near the sleepy fishing village that we call home, here on the Gulf Coast of Florida. Walking in one hot day, dressed in cutoffs and a pair of thongs after mowing my grass, I hurried to the teller window. In front of me waited a small wisp of a man, bent slightly, wearing a faded green sport shirt. His "skinnier-than-mine" legs dangled from a pair of too loose khaki hiking shorts.

He spoke softly to the young woman at the teller window: "I want a bank draft for thirty thousand dollars. I have found a property that I wish to purchase for an investment." The girl didn't even look up. Like Santa Claus, she "spoke not a word, but went straight to her work." After pressing one lever and consulting her computer, she wrote out the money order with no hesitancy.

I stepped to the window and whispered softly, "I want a bank draft for thirty thousand dollars. I need a Mercedes."

She sat straight up and roared with laughter. After she saw who I was, she said with a chortle, "Betty, you crazy lady! The difference between you and Mr. Miller—what most people haven't seen—is the fact that he has been making small deposits regularly for a long time. We are familiar with him and his assets, so that when he comes in and makes a large demand of us, we can meet his request."

Walking home I thought about this curious incident. True, the person I talk to most frequently on the phone is the one whose voice I will recognize most quickly. Our heavenly Father suggests that we pray without ceasing, and seek Him early. What spoiled children we are to think we can casually pass a few phrases upward and obtain the same powerful and unexplainable energy as the person who communicates with God on a regular basis.

Some of my best writing thoughts come during periods of "creative silence" as I reflect quietly on the Word—like Colossians 1:11: "Strengthened with all might, according to His glorious power . . . with joy." Joy is the undeniable sign of the presence of God. The "unction" and "anointing" of the Holy Spirit are those unseen components of strength, charisma and zeal that Samson tapped into when he grabbed the skeletal jawbone of a donkey and killed, single-handedly, one thousand heathen enemies of the living God.

Samson's story teaches us a lot about invisible strength and energy. When Manoah and his wife wanted a child, the angel of the Lord came and told her that she would bear a son. She was instructed to practice holiness, and to rear her son in the same manner (Judges 13). Holiness is essential to God's energy—an invisible virtue that brings visible results.

Samson was born and grew and "the Spirit of the Lord began to move upon him" (Judges 13:25). In chapter 14 we read that while he was traveling a lion roared against him. With his bare hands he tore up the lion. Later, when the Philistines, the enemy of God, roared against him, he destroyed their crops.

At one point in Samson's life, through Delilah's schemes, he came unplugged from the Source. Rendered helpless, he was blinded. After that he repented and returned to the Source. The day of his death he killed more enemies of God at one time than during his whole lifetime.

Satan can't steal your supernatural energy. That unseen strength is a bond between you and your God. Every Christian has a "dual" nature. You can learn as did Samson that who wins the "duel" depends on which nature you feed. With God's strength behind you, His love within you and His everlasting arms beneath you, you are more than sufficiently fortified for any days of trial ahead. We are living in perilous times. Do your best and God will make up the difference.

We don't get mail delivery in our little town. Everyone here walks to a tiny and friendly old building two blocks from the Gulf. The Twenty-third Psalm has become my formula for energy for those and other walks: "He restoreth my soul." (He restocks my shelves, recharges my battery, even overhauls my engine that I may hit on all twelve cylinders!) I was humming as I walked along recently, keeping step to the cadence of my own music. Now, I can't really sing, but I was enjoying it anyway. You don't write about a horrible experience while you are going through it—such as riding on the back of a wild horse or swooping down a turbulent river of rapids. As you read on, you can perhaps relate to the pit I had just emerged from. It was so good to be happy and to hear myself singing again.

Suddenly as I ducked to miss the overhang of Spanish moss, I came face to face on the narrow sidewalk with Harmless Harvey. Had I spotted him sooner I would have darted down the hiking path behind the post office, or crossed the street to avoid him. Harvey is a stocky old guy with a bulbous nose and a matching pouch just beneath his rib cage. He can consume more time communicating from his fertile imagination than any other male of any other age I have ever met. His brother who lives nearby says of him, "Harv lives a fantasy life. He embraces the sweet illusion that all the old ladies are chasing him!"

My husband, Carl, was on an extended stay in Rhode Island so I didn't really want to stop and talk to Harv. Now, don't misunderstand—I'm not afraid of him. Alcohol has slowed him down and he is old. But I just wasn't geared for a long conversation.

Showing his dentures he grinned a genuine smile and exclaimed, "I've been wanting to get you alone for a long time!" Now, no one has said that to me for thirty years! Then he asked, "What do you take? You're 'on' something. Nobody is that happy."

"I've had a faith lift," I reported with a smile.

"You should post the name of your cosmetic surgeon in public. He did a terrific job on your face. You sure look good!"

"No, Harvey," I said. "I don't lisp. I didn't say *face* lift, I said *faith* lift." His brother had asked Carl and me to share our faith with Harvey if the opportunity ever came to do so. Now seemed like a good time. I was rising to the challenge. I told Harvey that I had to pray every morning before I had the proper energy and motivation to tackle the day, and that Jesus was the Source of my joy.

During our conversation, I wondered if Harv would even remember our talk. It seemed he had been drinking heavily. But he showed up at church late the following Sunday night with his niece and her husband. When Ed Schlossmacher, who supplied the message in my

pastor husband's absence, gave the altar call, he challenged the
audience, "If you wish to be transformed by the power of the living
God, turn and kneel at your pew and talk to Him as you would to
your earthly father and tell Him what you need."

From my vantage point at the organ bench, I witnessed that Harv
was the first one to turn and kneel. Twenty minutes later when he
stood to leave, wiping his eyes with his handkerchief, I knew that
the unseen world had touched him. It was true. Our community is
seeing a man being restored to what God intended him to be.

I could radiate God's energy to him that previous Monday morning because I had experienced its reality. I am glad Harvey had not
met me two weeks previously. I had just come through some severe
storms, perhaps the most trying of my entire life, and if you have
read my other books, you know I'm a "survivor."

I have been depressed only once before. I experienced post-
surgical letdown after back surgery when doctors removed a tumor
from down inside my spinal column. But almost right up until the
time I talked with Harvey, the year had been a "wipeout" for me.
For starters, my husband had been restless the year before. He was
called to be a missionary when he was nineteen. His happiest years
were spent overseas in missions. When we moved from a three-
story Victorian house into our tiny four-room home, I tried for a
year to absorb Carl's anxieties. Even though the church had grown
since he became their shepherd, he missed missions and training
Bible school students for missionary work. He made the decision to
face a new mountain to climb for a while, working at Zion Bible
Institute in Barrington, Rhode Island.

My youngest daughter, April, was between colleges. She was
graduated from Wheaton College and had been accepted for her
master's work in physical therapy, but was also restless in the
months of waiting to start. She took a job in Gainesville, Florida,
just blocks from where hideous murders of five students occurred.
She rarely slept, living alone there, driving to and from her job in
constant fear. She told me, "I pray and read Scripture, but some-

times, Mother, I lie awake and look at the ceiling.'' We had been concerned for her safety.

Then she had trauma of another kind. While she was enjoying a ride on our Seadoo (sit-down jet ski for two) the 385-pound craft hit a four-foot swell and flew straight up. As April fell off the back, the directional fin and exhaust landed on her and tore deeply into her leg. I suffered with her during her painful recovery.

Then there was the time I lay in bed for fifteen days with high fever and pneumonia. During this time my editors returned the first draft of this manuscript and asked for a total rewrite. They detected a cloud of depression on my work, and thoughtfully suggested that I get my health and vitality tracking before tackling the work. On top of everything else, our cars had serious, expensive breakdowns.

I have learned from an older conqueror, ''When you get depressed, give something away, quickly.'' I tried it. My family loves for me to bake them an angel food cake. At that point even the dial on my mixer, the Oster Kitchen Center, was depressing. The indicator could be set at whip, mix, beat or blend. I felt personally that my ''inner mixer'' could be labeled mashed, slashed, crushed and squelched.

As soon as I removed the cake from the oven to cool, I realized I had to get alone with God and ask Him to restore my soul. It was Wednesday. Since I was born on Wednesday, I had decided a while back to declare it a weekly holiday, a midweek day for prayer, meditation, creative silence, even having some fun. No wonder I was running out of gas. I had ignored my need for a time apart. I had not taken time to plug into the Source. I was running out of energy before my task was completed because I had not waited at the pump long enough to get a full tank of fuel.

When will I learn that when this happens I need to stop and evaluate? To ask myself: Am I exhausted because I am doing more than God intended me to do, or because I am not taking His power to do it with?

Grabbing my pelican beach towel with heavy hands, crying so hard I could barely see to get down the steps to the garage, I put a bottle of water and sack lunch in the car, and started driving south toward Dunedin's Caladesi Causeway and Honeymoon Island. I had been so busy worrying about my family, working and writing, I had forgotten to enjoy this little paradise I live so close to.

Honeymoon Island, before the bridge was built, was accessible only by boat. They called it Honeymoon Island because poor grovers who picked fruit in the citrus groves were awarded 24 hours alone over there to celebrate their marriages. The next day, "boss man" would send a boat to bring them back to work again.

My car is an old restored 1962 MGA convertible. It is dark British racing green with spoke wheels. Since we have done some work on it, it hums and purrs and we get 37 miles to the gallon. Driving along in this old friend, I tried to think of God's love for me. I could hardly turn the steering wheel, my hands felt so weighed down. "Restore to me the joy of my salvation," I prayed. "Clear my mental computer and help me to rejoice again."

I wore dark glasses so no one could see my red, swollen eyes. It was ninety degrees out, so they could think the water running down my face was perspiration instead of salty, bitter, stinging tears that I could not control. It felt as though a dam had broken inside of me.

Arriving at the guard gate, I showed my pass and drove numbly to the parking area. There were very few cars there yet, in the early morning sun, so I pulled into the third parking spot since my favorite number is three. Taking a light folding chair from the trunk of the car I started walking, walking, walking. The dark cloud in my spirit had robbed me of a most gorgeous sunrise. I tried to quote Scripture. "Jesus said, 'My grace is sufficient for you.' "

"But barely," I moaned.

I tried to sing. The only song I could think of was "Hiding in Thee," and the only verse that made sense was the one that contained this assessment:

> How oft in the conflict when pressed by the foe,
> Have I run to my refuge and breathed out my woe.

So that is what I did—breathed out my woe!

I tried to reason with myself, "You've had a fair amount of success in the past, writing, speaking, helping others. Your bills are paid." I recalled a verse: "David comforted himself *in the Lord.*" I realized I could not do it by myself.

I began walking on the edge of the water, splashing, sending the cool spray up into the sunshine. Before I realized it, I had walked the three miles to the end of the island. I slumped into my little folding chair while the warm sun penetrated the muscles in my shoulders. Looking out over the white sand and the surf, I spotted four porpoises rolling and playing, close in, just for my benefit.

When I was thirsty I drank from the plastic bottle, and when I finally got a bit of an appetite, I opened the sack. I had put a sandwich, a banana and a leftover fortune cookie in there. We had been to a Chinese restaurant several days before, and I had not opened the cookie for the little message insert. Now, I don't "bank" on fortune cookies and the sort, but strangely enough when I opened it and read, "Nature, time and patience are the three great physicians," I was amazed at the timing.

I mused on this. God created nature, a beautiful world for us to enjoy. He started time and will declare when time shall be no more. Patience is a virtue that only Jesus and His sanctifying power can accomplish in a naturally energetic personality like mine. It reminded me that the Word states that Jesus is *the* Great Physician. He can heal bodies and situations, too.

Sitting on that beach with no timepiece, it seemed I had lost track of time. I found myself looking back to my miracle resurrection experience when Jesus the Great Physician not only healed me, but gave me a foretaste of His resurrection power. I became a literal representative of His resurrection power and love to tell about it.

There in the warm sun and gentle ocean breeze I closed my eyes and recalled how the nurse had phoned my family from the hospital to tell them that I had died. The doctor had signed the death certificate and covered me with a sheet. The events from that point began unfolding in a beautiful panorama.

During those 28 minutes of death, I walked through a meadow of waving grass. Each blade was like an individual strand of soft green velvet. I saw flowers exactly like those you may have in your own back yard, and I also saw flowers that I have never seen here, in colors and quality I cannot describe.

I walked—or perhaps ran—uphill effortlessly, alongside the wall of a city, the capital of the ''country'' of heaven. The ninth layer of stone around the wall was topaz, my November birthstone. I had not, before this experience, read the book of Revelation that describes this city, but I saw it! It is built according to the architectural specifications laid out in chapter 21 of the book of Revelation.

My escort was a tall, tall angel. I used to think angels were effeminate. After seeing that masculine being I think that no more.

Heaven was a natural place, and the people I saw, whom I knew on earth before their own deaths, were still themselves, but they were glorified in mind and body. They knew me and I knew them.

Heaven was a place of worship, singing and service. Heaven's work is as free from care, toil and fatigue as the wingstroke of the jubilant lark when it soars into the sunlight and pours out its thrilling carol. Work up there is a matter of desire as well as a matter of obedience to the ruling will of God. It is work according to one's tastes, delight and ability. Tastes vary there, and occupations vary. If you were overworked here, heaven will be a place of eternal rest from your labors.

After seeing the flowers, I know that florists will love their occupation. There is no backache, toil, sweat, thorn, thistle or bug to destroy the blossom's beauty. Farmers will harvest without planting. I believe that God took seeds out of paradise and transplanted them in Eden, so we could know what it is like there.

Back in Union Hospital, my dad was so heartbroken he stood by my bed and sobbed *Jesus*. He moaned that name to comfort himself, but in that one-word prayer, he wished that I had not died. I never wanted to leave that glorious place, but hearing him utter that name changed my mind. Returning to my body—not much of a body since I weighed only 68 pounds upon my return—I experienced resurrection. I saw the Word written in light and coming to me. It was John 11:25: "I am the resurrection, and the life: he that believeth in me, though he were dead, yet shall he live" (KJV). I touched the Word and sat up, very much alive.

I was amazed at how many earthly features I saw in heaven, and upon returning, realized how much of heaven's eternal quality is in this lovely world, and in people here.

My friend Mona Johnian and her husband direct a teaching center in Winchester, Massachusetts. They have done extensive research on heaven, and I have asked her to help me describe what I saw there.

Paradise, like Eden, is an orchard and a forest, lush and green. God has created us for this very thing. In 2 Corinthians 5:1–5, as Mona puts it, "Paul tells us that when we lose this body, we have eternal residence in heaven, immediate and quick."

It is a big, multi-faceted place, where you will never be bored. God's presence is there. So are the tree of life, fruit, peace, joy, beauty, work, truth, animals, trees, flowers and total absence of death. This is described in the book of Hebrews.

Mona believes that Genesis 2:5–8 tells us God planted a garden and transplanted it from heaven to earth. The gardens in heaven must be glorious indeed! In the midst of this paradise is God's throne. There is a tree that bears twelve varieties of fruit and there is no winter there, for the tree bears a fresh crop every month. Revelation 22:1 tells us that out of the throne of that celestial city flows a pure river, the river of life.

What a boost to dip in the water of life, to splash life onto your body, into every pore of your skin! You can dip in and drink a glass of life, or bathe in eternal, living water. Here on earth people drink a toast to life; there we will be *drinking* life.

The leaves of the tree of life are for the healing of the nations. Imagine nibbling a healing leaf, nibbling healing and health, just to ensure that life is to last forever! Everywhere you turn, you will be looking at, walking in life!

Paul wrote in Philippians 3:13 not to look back, but this was one

case where it was good for me to look back and recall that miracle.
Jesus' name worked for me in 1959; I reasoned that it must work
again for me now in 1990 in this horrible pit into which I had fallen.
"At the name of Jesus every knee shall bow" (Philippians 2:10).
Even the knee of depression must bow at His name. I could hardly
say anything aloud at first. My voice was weak, but I moaned *Jesus*
over and over again.

I had no idea what time it was. Who cared? I had prayed, "Show
me Your glory," and He was doing just that! Scriptures came to my
mind: "One day with the Lord is as a thousand years," "Every
good and perfect gift comes down from God above," "Joy cometh
in the morning," and I recalled a song:

> Some golden daybreak, Jesus will come,
> Some golden daybreak when battles are won.
> We'll shout the victory, break through the blue
> Some golden daybreak for me . . . for you.

There is no sickness, no stress, not a sorrow on earth that heaven
can't heal in the morning of joy! This quote was about eternity, but
the invisible world had touched me prematurely! What a morning I
had experienced!

Watching two pelicans swoop and soar, I felt that if the joy of the
Lord were intensified any more, I would be raptured on that sandy,
sunny, breezy spot! I believe that when Jesus comes again this is
what will actually happen. His power and joy will so intensify that
we will be translated to His place.

By now the sun was intense and people were filling the island. I
strolled back toward the main beach lazily and peacefully. I met an
older man who asked, "Did you have a good walk?"

"Yes, sir! But I must warn you, it's farther coming back than
going out." (I had my sense of humor back!)

And then back to the real world of husbands and kitchens, I
headed toward the parking lot and the drive home. Those few
hours with the Creator and His creation were holy insulation from

the perilous times of the past and those that may come in the future. I had been and still am fortified with His energy and joy. I had "sipped eternity." The timeless unseen world to come had touched me!

Driving home I sang loudly, " 'Tis so sweet to trust in Jesus, just to take Him at His Word. . . . Oh, for grace to trust Him more."

My old MGA has a noisy muffler, so no one but the Lord heard my gusto. I was singing again. The energy from the invisible world had come to me as instantaneously and miraculously as the dazzling light that shafted down to Saul and turned him around.

I sang on. . . .

> He brought me out of the miry clay . . .
> He set my feet on the Rock to stay . . .
> He puts a song in my soul today . . .
> A song of praise, Hallelujah!
> I'll tell of the pit with its gloom and despair,
> I'll praise the dear Father who answered my prayer,
> I'll praise my Redeemer who has rescued me.
> He brought me out!

The Scripture that this song is taken from is Psalm 40:2–3: "He also brought me up out of a horrible pit . . . and set my feet upon a rock. . . . He has put a new song in my mouth—praise to our God."

I thought of a little story about that pit:

A man fell into a pit and couldn't get himself out.

A subjective person came along and said, "I feel for you, down there."

An objective person came along and said, "It's logical that someone would fall down there."

A Pharisee said, "Only bad people fall into pits."

A mathematician calculated how he fell into the pit.

A fundamentalist said, "You deserve your pit."

An I.R.S. agent asked if he was paying taxes in his pit.

A self-pitying person said, "You haven't seen anything until you've seen my pit!"

A charismatic said, "Just confess that you're not in the pit."

An optimist said, "Things could be worse."

A pessimist said, "Things *will* get worse."

Jesus said, "Take My hand," and lifted him out of the pit!

After my return home, during dinner, I shared the account of my day with my husband. He must have picked up on the afterglow of my experience. When we finished eating, he suggested that we go together down to the boat dock and watch the sunset. It was just going down, touching the water's surface like a red-orange ball.

We sat together on a rock beneath a huge old mossy oak tree and watched until it melted like golden butter on the horizon and streamed across the water's glassy surface all the way to us on shore. It looked like the golden boulevard that runs through the center of the celestial city! No wonder Peter could attempt to walk on the water. Seeing Jesus in person could not have revealed His presence any more than we felt that evening looking at His glory! I knew in part what the thousand years of peace mentioned in the book of Revelation will be like—bliss!

There is a supernatural energy available to all of us through creative silence. This generation is a noisy generation. It has been pumped, primed and hyped. We are being stirred, but not changed. We are being entertained temporarily, but not receiving lasting strength. There is a lot of energy projected in religious television productions. Some are reaching the unchurched, but I see a danger. As I travel around the country I see pastors striving to become Christian movie stars and expending a lot of time and money to transform their churches into religious theaters of the performing arts. It is possible to be stimulated and entertained without absorbing the Holy Spirit's energy to produce long-lasting fruit for the Master and His Kingdom to come.

God created Adam in His image. I believe that image-man Adam was formed perfectly in body and mind, and was energized daily as he walked with the creative Source of invisible energy from the unseen Kingdom. Adam returned with Eve to the Source, God, in the cool of the latter part of the day. Adam was formed from the earth, tilled the earth and survived from the nutrition he consumed from the earth.

Marjorie Kinnan Rawlings, author of the book *Cross Creek*, has put it this way: "The first man was a part of the earth before men were a part of the womb." She had lost her creative energy to write in the noise of New York City and came to a quiet cabin in a citrus grove near Cross Creek in mid-state Florida. In this place she completed several novels, two of which have been made into movies that are still popular.

Gene Stratton Porter was energized by the Limberlost, the wooded wetlands and bird sanctuaries of southern Indiana. She wrote thirteen classics, including *The Girl of the Limberlost* and *Freckles*.

I was born and grew up near her spot. When I was a small girl, my dad pastored a church in the beautiful hills of southwestern Indiana. We did not live in the parsonage provided by the church. Our parents bought a little farm where my four brothers and I could have a horse, a dog, a cat, and hit a baseball without breaking out a neighbor's window. *And* where we could know God through the earth. We always had a garden and flowers.

A worn and weary missionary friend of our family had just returned to the States from the Philippines where he had constructed a Bible school. Totally bankrupt of strength, he sought sanctuary in our humble country home.

Early one morning in May, I was awakened by the roar of a tractor motor just as the sun was coming up. Later when it pulled out of the field I could see a warm vapor from the freshly plowed loamy soil meeting the rays of the early morning sun. Then I saw our missionary friend walk slowly to the field and lie down in a newly made furrow, the cradle of God's earth, and look up at the sky.

Later that evening at dinner I noticed that he was cheerful and so much better. He ate heartily. From then on, he began to recover and was ready to work again in a few short days.

I asked him about it and he explained, "I had to do something. When I smelled the warm fragrance coming from the plowed earth, I remembered how Marjorie Rawlings had said that Adam was a part of the earth. As I rested in the substance of creation, the dust from which God created man, He re-energized, recreated, restored me. Lying there I worshiped God the Creator and Jesus who suffered to heal me. I remembered parts of Psalm 34: 'Oh, magnify the Lord with me, and let us exalt His name together. I sought the Lord, and He heard me, and delivered me from all my fears. They looked to Him and were radiant. . . . This poor man cried out, and the Lord heard him, and saved him out of all his troubles. The angel of the Lord encamps all around those who fear Him, and delivers them.' " Invisible energy came to him, and I appreciated the story most of all after being filled in my own time of need.

I have always liked the story of Elisha because he received a *double* portion of supernatural energy from the unseen world. He was willing to wait, according to Elijah's instructions, until he received God's creative power. He remained full of this power from the Holy Spirit during his life and even retrained it after he was dead and buried. Second Kings 13:21 tells that once when a funeral was in progress they put the man in the tomb of Elisha; and when the body was let down and touched the bones of Elisha, he revived and stood on his feet.

I remember with tenderness an old song:

> Shut in with God in a secret place,
> There in the Spirit beholding His face,
> Gaining new power to run in life's race,
> I long to be shut in with God.

It was Amiel who wrote in his old classic *The Inner Life* that talent consists in appearing to be what we are inside. The only substance properly so called is the invisible soul, the spirit to become what God wants us to be with reward. With Him, we become *grand* with His universe. The visits from the Holy Spirit are sufficient to fill us with enthusiasm.

There is invisible energy in the spoken Word. Try it. Read aloud the following condensed version in lovely King James English of Isaiah 40:

> Comfort ye my people. . . . She hath received of the Lord's hand double for all her sins. . . . Every valley shall be exalted, and every mountain and hill shall be made low: and the crooked shall be made straight, and the rough places plain. And the glory of the Lord shall be revealed, . . . for the mouth of the Lord hath spoken it. . . . The grass withereth, . . . because the spirit of the Lord bloweth upon it: . . . but the word of our God shall stand for ever. . . . Behold your God! . . . He shall feed his flock like a shepherd: he shall gather the lambs with his arm, and carry them in his bosom.
>
> Who hath directed the Spirit of the Lord, or being his counselor hath taught him? . . . Hast thou not known? hast thou not heard, that the everlasting God . . . fainteth not, neither is weary? . . . He giveth power [unseen energy] to the faint; and to them that have no might he increaseth strength.

After Jesus' death and resurrection, His disciples were drained and shut in behind closed doors. He came to them and taught them a lesson on invisible energy. They were a great team with a dream for the world and the Kingdom to come, but they had run out of steam. Jesus breathed on them and said, "Receive the Holy Spirit" (John 20:22).

Christians today are blue because they are breathing improperly. They give out more than they are breathing in, so they set themselves up to "pass out" spiritually. Wait in His presence, let Him breathe supernatural life into you. Nothing we can acquire on earth can compare with the invisible energy of His Kingdom. It is ready for you. Take time to receive it.

3

SEEING THE INVISIBLE WORLD THROUGH EYES OF FAITH

I became a widow at the age of 27. My husband died during open heart surgery at the J. Hillis Miller Center in Gainesville, Florida, leaving me lonely, heartbroken and pregnant with our second baby. I survived on Social Security and bouillon cubes, alone with my two little girls, for six years.

I wanted a loving, godly husband to share the rest of my life. I prayed, I window-shopped and I had friendly "agents" among my relatives and friends gawking for me, too. I dated five different men during those six years, going out to dinner, fixing lunch for them, sitting with a gentleman occasionally at a concert or in church.

One day I read a familiar Bible verse with new insight: "Faith is the *substance* of things hoped for, the evidence of things not seen" (Hebrews 11:1). I had faith, but I needed substance—something, someone to hold, someone to see, to feel, to communicate with.

So I did something. I went to Maas Brothers Department Store and bought a soft black lace gown and tucked it away in my cedar chest even though I didn't yet have a husband to wear it for! A few days later, my oldest daughter, Brenda, was looking for linens to change the beds and shrieked, "What's this?" I explained to her and we both had a good laugh together.

Very soon after our chat, during youth choir, Brenda met a girl, Connie, whose mother had died with cancer. Connie, whom I had not met, walked up to me at Vacation Bible School and said, "I'd like to have you for my mother. May I introduce you to my dad?" Her dad and I have now been married nineteen years.

It is a great mystery to me how our actions can bolster our faith. "Doing something" can somehow take us a step deeper into that unseen world. Let's look at another example—a life-and-death example—and see what conclusions we can draw.

Ed and Ruth Schlossmacher watched through the glass window of the isolation room while a team of skilled physicians fought desperately to save their four-year-old son's life. The day before, "Little Ed" had refused to eat, his temperature had elevated and by evening he was moaning with pain. They rushed him to Children's Hospital in Buffalo, New York, where he was diagnosed with spinal meningitis.

These frightened parents watched the doctors work feverishly over their little boy. His fever had reached 106 degrees and his little body shook uncontrollably. A grim fact was written on the doctors' faces . . . that this was a life-and-death struggle. Finally, one doctor emerged from behind the glass window into the hallway and suggested that Ed and Ruth go home to get some rest. They left reluctantly after he assured them that he would call if there was any change.

Driving home slowly, Ed and Ruth talked to each other and talked to God aloud together: "Please, God, don't let Edward die." Their wills and minds took posts on an unseen battleground—their desire for him to live, their willingness to let go of that desire if God's will was really for him to die. They had presented their baby boy to the Lord in dedication a few days following his birth, and hoped someday that he might follow his father's calling and become a minister. How were they to pray and believe?

En route home, they passed the church in South Buffalo where they were pastoring. Cars were in the parking lot and members were inside praying for their little boy to be healed. What a comfort the family of God is when trouble strikes!

Arriving home about nine P.M. they had hardly gotten in the door when the phone rang. It was a nurse. "Hurry back to the hospital. Your son is dying." Returning to the hospital, they raced through the streets, praying all the way as they drove, "O God, please let them be wrong."

At the hospital, the grim verdict of the physicians was confirmed. In spite of this, a strange peace from the unseen world suddenly descended on Ed and settled on him. He recalled the personal words of Jesus spoken to Jairus when his little daughter had died: "Be not afraid, only believe." Jairus did believe and his daughter was literally raised from the dead. Ed knew then how to pray. He and Ruth would believe in faith for their son's healing.

The following morning Little Ed was still alive, but the doctor presented discouraging news. Testing indicated that there had been permanent brain damage caused by high fever over an extended period of time. "Should he survive, he might never walk or talk. If he lives at all he might never come out of this coma."

Ed and Ruth did not give up. They clung to the lifeline of prayer for his healing. Did the doctor not realize that the only reason he was alive was due to their holding on in prayer? The couple prayed, "Edward has always been Yours, Lord. And if You want him to bloom in heaven, it's all right with us. But we ask You to heal him. And if You do, he is still Yours." This was not a passiveness, not neutrality, not defeated resignation. It was loving relinquishment. They had learned that when your mind and the mind of Christ are the same, *nothing can stop you.*

Driving home, Ruth was crying, but faith had reached her heart and she, too, felt peace. Like a flash, Ed felt this impression: *Do something. Go home and paint the tricycle.* In response to that voice of faith, he bought red enamel and they began sanding and painting the tricycle that someone had recently given them. That project became a point of contact for their faith. As he worked, Ed fixed a "faith picture" in his heart. He "saw" the little fellow pedaling fast, up and down the sidewalk, well and strong!

A few days later they learned that there was a slight change for the better. The medical staff moved Little Ed into a cubicle in the children's ward where his parents could touch their comatose son and talk to him. During the days they sat by his bed, and at night they worked on the tricycle. On the twelfth day, Edward awoke. He recognized his parents and talked to them. The nurse quickly brought jello and Ruth fed it to her son! They laughed and cried and praised the Lord all at the same time.

It was the beginning of a complete recovery. He had been in the hospital for 22 days. Before releasing him the hospital specialists tested his brain and were unable to find any damage. As the family left the hospital the attending physician declared with a broad smile, "There goes a miracle!"

That evening with great joy they lifted Edward onto the seat of his red tricycle. Soon thereafter the Buffalo *News* ran an article attributing this miraculous recovery to prayer, since that type of meningitis is one hundred percent fatal.

Young Edward gave his life to Christ at an early age. He excelled in high school and received a full scholarship to the Illinois Institute of Technology in Chicago. He was on the dean's list all four years and was made a member of two honor societies. Not bad for permanent brain damage! He married Joy Hartman and completed his doctoral studies in chemical engineering at Princeton University. Later a missionary spirit began to burn in Ed's heart, taking him to Puerto Rico and Japan for ministry there. Ed and Joy are now fully appointed missionaries with a special assignment in Japan.

As E.D. Howe wrote recently in *Pentecostal Evangel*, sometimes during a storm it is possible for winds of discouragement and self-pity to blow you right out of the will of God. But if you act as if it's impossible to fail, God will see that you come through it. This is illustrated over and over throughout Scripture. Our faith is what He is searching for. Our faith can move the heart of Jesus.

Many people are "too smart" to understand the principle of faith.

It requires childlike believing, a heart unafraid to trust Jesus. This says to me that there is a veil covering the unseen world that only a child can understand and tear away! Faith is the invisible energy that produces visible results as we act on the belief that God is our good Father and that He wants to lead us into His good will.

Stubbornness that dictates what must happen is not faith. Rather, it is perseverance that pursues our desires. It is as if you write a letter to your heavenly Father. Faith in your heart here on earth ascends to the invisible Kingdom of God in heaven. As He opens the seal of your heart's desire, His Father-heart responds not only to your need, but to the fact that you trust Him to respond. He never lets that kind of letter go unanswered.

I am amazed at how many people won't have faith in the invisible world, but have faith in almost anything else. They think God is dead, yet believe Elvis Presley is alive. They don't trust the Bible, yet will believe that Elvis has been spotted at the airport. Just for the record, the Bible is the only material object we have that we can actually say is eternal—not people or places (see Mark 13:31).

Be careful not to confuse cocky command with the quiet power of assurance. I received a humorous letter from another writer while writing this chapter. He said, "I thought if I just ordered tapes from those faith people in Tulsa, I could talk God into anything, bring my fondest desires into existence. I went around as a new baby Christian hanging out my diapers in public. Before I got 'into the Word' I thought that Jacob's ladder descended from heaven to Tulsa!"

Thank God for leaders who have taught us that we do not have to live in poverty to be spiritual. They have warmed up a lot of "funeral churches" and inspired droopy Christians to kick their negative habits. But at the same time there is no substitute for digging your own private wellspring, exercising your faith by reading the Word, stretching your muscles by believing. Too long this lazy generation has been running around the country looking for a shortcut to answered prayer, some bit of knowledge from the lips of a religious palmreader or Christian fortune-teller who is seeking to build his own magic kingdom instead of lifting up Jesus and His Kingdom to come.

There are three kinds of believers: the unbeliever, the make-believer and the true believer. The Word declares, "If you can believe, you *will* see the glory of God. He who has begun a good work in you shall also complete it."

What a deal we have as believers in Jesus, the Author and Finisher of our faith (Hebrews 12:2)! He gives us working capital by the Holy Spirit, instructs us how to invest it and then makes it happen, and completes the transaction to our great satisfaction! We children of God can't lose.

You may be reading this and thinking, *I don't have any faith.* I am a firm believer that we have equal opportunity through prayer. You *do* have faith: "God has dealt to each one a measure of faith" (Romans 12:3). If you lick the back of a stamp, for instance, you have faith to believe that when you stick that tiny piece of paper onto an envelope, a red, white and blue truck, complete with driver, will take your letter to the airport where a pilot will fly a million-dollar plane to its destination. And it will arrive on time, if you have faith to mail it five days in advance of the date you want it to arrive.

You do have faith. When you walk into a dark room and reach for a tiny plastic switch, that's faith. The dark will flee and you can light up a whole room. When you push a tiny silver key into the ignition of your four-cylinder car, you are witnessing your faith at work.

Probably the best illustration is that by scribbling your signature at the bottom right corner of a piece of paper just two and one-half by six inches, you by faith transform that check into a sandwich, groceries or a beautiful home (if, like Mr. Miller, you have made deposits!).

Your faith may be small, but invest what you have. When your faith touches the unseen world, you embrace God. The temporary becomes permanent; the weak merges with strong; the invisible becomes visible. You do not need a formula when you have the Father. He gives wisdom to those who ask, and if the supply for your need is not on earth, He can send it from heaven. If it does not exist, He can create it. If it has never been done, He can do it.

We strain at finding God's will. If we just seek Him, God's will will find us. Faith is looking for us. God's creative love and power are leaning toward us. The Lord's Prayer bears out this simple fact: "Thy will be done, [as easily and simply] on earth as it is in heaven." He will accomplish whatever concerns you and me (Psalm 138:8). He is our Provider, our strong Nourisher, our unseen Source.

Jesus talked about "mustard-seed faith." The mustard is the tiniest of seeds, but the tree grows to twelve feet at maturity. Your faith may be small, but plant what you have. Don't wear your mustard seed around your neck! Plant it, invest it, do something with it. A weight-lifter does not pump five hundred pounds of iron the first day of his workout. He starts with ten pounds on each arm and builds from there. After his faith in his ability and his body grow, he can lift five hundred pounds.

I know a woman who is a worrier. Each night she writes her concerns down on a piece of paper, then throws the list into the wastepaper basket beside her bed. She commits it to God, who neither slumbers nor sleeps. She reasons, "If God is going to be awake, there is no need for me to stay awake and worry." This is one clear and simple approach to faith. Here is another.

One godly man told me, "Because of my work with investments, my schedule is hectic. So each morning, before I leave home, I have Communion. I partake of a small piece of bread and a sip of grape juice. This reminder of the Last Supper and Jesus provides a symbolic substance for strength. It gives me steady and constant stability all day. Jesus' body assures me that He will take care of my physical needs and help me resist temptation and evil. His blood reminds me that if I fall, His blood will atone for my sin."

I was speaking at a women's retreat a couple of years ago and the directors of that conference informed me that the four hundred registered guests were all of diverse backgrounds. Some were pastors' wives, frustrated from being expected to do more than they were capable of performing. Some were single women, facing loneliness. Others were businesswomen, weary from the competition of the workplace.

I knelt in prayer and asked, "Lord, give me the prescription to meet their needs, so multiple, so complex. When You were on earth, You gravitated toward need. From where You sit, Jesus, at the right hand of God, You are totally aware of the best plan for me to follow."

An idea, smarter than I am, surfaced in my mind. I constructed a crude replica of Jesus' cross from two rough planks of wood, and laid it on the altar in the front of the auditorium. Then when the women had gathered, I gave each of them a piece of red paper, symbolic of the blood of Jesus. I reminded them how Jesus' blood had flowed freely from the cross of Calvary to cleanse our sins, heal our sickness; how His blood paid the final price for all our needs.

I asked them to write down their deepest personal needs on the red paper and I read from Colossians 2, how Jesus made peace through the blood of His cross to reconcile all things, whether they be in earth or in heaven. And we are complete in Him who is the head of all principalities and powers, blotting out the handwriting of ordinances against us. He took that which was contrary to us, and nailed it to *His* cross. And having spoiled principalities and powers, He triumphed over them.

It was a moving, humbling sight, those four hundred women, red paper in hand, upon which they had written their most heartfelt needs. By each side of the cross I placed a hammer and small nails. Praying silently as they came, they nailed their needs to His cross and left them there, praising aloud as they went back to their seats, thanking God in advance for the answer that was on the way. They had used their credit cards of faith and hope took hold of each of us. With the sound of the hammer they imagined God, their unseen Father, receiving their petition and by the eye of faith they believed that He would hear their requests and answer their prayers.

I am still getting letters reporting answers to those prayers. We invested our simple faith in a symbolic exercise and God heard us.

These are perilous times. War clouds scudded over our peaceful America. Another serious earthquake is being predicted. Droughts and famines plague our world. As playwright William Saroyan penned, "There's a sorrow in the nature of things." The world is negative, but Jesus said, "Fear not, I have overcome the world."

Have you noticed how most pulls are downward? Take the weather report: ten percent chance of rain. Why not report the ninety percent chance of sunshine? And why call it a "stop" light? It is only one-third stop, one-third caution and one-third *go*. Newspaper and television reports generally record a fraction of what is happening to a fraction of people. Most of the time they report only the negative. God is still in charge of the unseen government. Faith in that world is a faith that reaches.

I have a new "Reach" toothbrush. The advertisement claims: "It can reach places where the ordinary toothbrush cannot go." Faith is like this. It can go into new areas. It can reach out and take hold of substance that we cannot yet see. "I found it necessary to write to you exhorting you to contend earnestly for the faith which was once for all delivered to the saints" (Jude 3).

We must not be satisfied with watered-down faith. We must contend for the brand of faith that Abraham, Isaac, Daniel and the woman with the issue of blood had . . . *reaching* faith.

4

PENETRATING THE INVISIBLE WORLD WITH PRAYER

*P*rayer is the unseen force that brings visible results. It is like an escalator by which we can ascend directly to the unseen world. It is a Holy Spirit power-driven set of stairs on an endless belt that goes toward heaven, continuously, never stopping, always on an upward course.

Webster's defines an escalator as "never standing still." To escalate is to increase in extent, formation, volume, number, amount, intensity and scope. *That's prayer!*

God in the beginning made man, created for him a heart and soul, and gave him the ability to commune and exchange thoughts with almighty God Himself. God initiated this divine plan because He wanted to communicate with us on a higher level. He planted a need in us to want this communication also. Think of it: Your heart is linked with His heart through prayer! Your soul is linked with His soul by the secure cable of your praying.

While writing *Prayers that Are Answered*, I learned that prayer is not conquering God's reluctance, but laying hold of His willingness. Prayer is not worrying out loud. Prayer is not idle chatter, reading pious words, mumbling into our mattress at bedtime or reciting our want lists. Genuine prayer is a learned skill; it can be a spiritual technique of warfare. Prayer that invades Satan's territory, that penetrates the second heaven (his domain) is an activity of the Holy Spirit. And it is hard work. Prayer warriors operate in "big leagues." Jesus, while on earth, sometimes prayed all night. Prayer is a dedicated vocation that requires long hours (the agony). But the joy comes when we grow energized through our praying and receive answers (the ecstasy).

People who are seeking the invisible Kingdom of God pray differently from the fickle masses who seek God in times of trouble and forget Him when the trouble passes. True believers show that their hearts can see into eternity! They pray with an authenticity of the heart that moves God.

"How-to" books on prayer are popular, especially if the focus is praying for personal wants. I was taught to pray at age two—I learned to pray at 42, and am still learning. In this chapter I want us to mature together, knowing that the same great God who cares about our small needs is still in charge of nations. Stretch with me from the whispered one-word prayer *Jesus* to the "big league" of praying for nations and breaking through enemy barriers.

We live in a marvelous age. I believe God is right now putting together a brand-new modern book of Acts as real and alive as the book by that same name in the New Testament.

Have you prayed recently and wondered if your distress signals were too weak to get through? Heaven's two-way communication system surpasses the most intricate wonders that even creators of space probes can devise! Our communication with the throne of heaven travels at high speed, and never once is a message garbled or lost. God registers the reaching, searching, needing message above the words we say.

Halfway through this book, I reached a plateau. I was fatigued physically and "burned out." The fascination had fizzled for me, and the subject matter had lost its lustre. At that point I heard my own weak and pitiful voice whining for help. I decided not to go to

Wednesday night prayer meeting, but stay home and apply myself to the task at hand. . . .

When the phone rang, the voice on the other end was the church secretary to remind me that they needed me to play the organ for the service. As I backed the car out the driveway somewhat reluctantly my neighbor called out to me, "Betty, how're you doing with your writing?"

"My computer's constipated," I replied honestly. "I feel like a woman whose pregnancy has lasted more than nine months. I'm heavy with this baby and want deliverance." We both laughed and I drove on to church.

After the service when most everyone had left, I did not talk to anyone but knelt quietly at a pew to talk to God, to rest in the Lord and wait patiently for Him. (I have learned one thing: that the energy of creative silence in His presence stimulates my knowledge.)

I had not even had time to whisper the first word in prayer when I felt a light arm around my shoulder. Opening my eyes only partially, with my head still bowed, I recognized Kelly Munn. Kelly is a teenager who attends our church, and she whispered an amazing prayer: "Lord, I love Betty. Help her finish her book. Resurrect her brain. Amen."

What a strange prayer! How did she know?

As I left the exit door toward the parking lot, she was waiting alone for me. "I apologize for that stupid prayer," she confessed.

"Kelly, you have no idea how appropriate it really was. I appreciate your loving concern. Thank you very much."

Arriving home, I fell wearily into bed and dropped into a sound sleep. I always sleep nine hours soundly, but that night I awakened at 1:15 A.M. fully rested, wide awake, energy flowing. I sat up in bed with my clipboard and wrote the skeleton for the next two chapters. I wrote so rapidly my pen smoked. (Well, almost!) I fell back to sleep around 4:00 and rested wonderfully until 8:05, when I was up and ready to go again!

God had answered that "strange" prayer. He had resurrected my brain and energized me through a girl's simple prayer of concern.

When you pray, Jesus becomes your editor, your attorney, your advocate. Even if you pray inappropriately, if your motive is pure, your shabby prayer is answered. Jesus takes your words, spoken or unspoken, screens them through your heart's motive and does not present them to His Father, and your Father, in that golden throne room until they are in their purest form. "But He, because He continues forever, has an unchangeable priesthood. Therefore He is also able to save to the uttermost those who come to God through Him, since He always lives to make intercession for them" (Hebrews 7:24–25). When someone is praying for you, God's mercy and light from the invisible Kingdom will find you and shine into your dark, searching heart.

Saul, later renamed Paul, learned this. He thought he was doing his people a favor by trying to rid them of the Christian population. God did *him* a favor, sent a blinding, revealing light in response to those Christians' prayers, and Saul turned about-face. He explained it this way: "I obtained mercy because I did it ignorantly in unbelief" (1 Timothy 1:13).

I thrilled at a modern Saul/Paul story.

Kevin Shorey told me that once when he was on a flight toward Oklahoma, he had to know why the young woman seated next to him was so radiantly joyous. She shared her discovery with him.

She had been involved in a horrible wreck, her back crushed. Lying on the highway before she had passed into unconsciousness, she had screamed out to Buddha for help. She told Kevin, "Buddha never showed up, but Jesus did! He talked to me; I talked to Him. He gave me a choice. I chose Him and life. He promised to take care of me."

In intensive care, the doctors told her and the family that she would be a quadriplegic evermore, paralyzed from her neck down. She shook her head no. She told them, "Even though I said words to Buddha because they were the only prayers I had been taught, my heart was searching for the true and living God. Jesus came in mercy. He came to me and told me I would be all right." In one month she was walking again!

We, as believers, are armed with the *only* power that is effective in the spiritual realm against the headquarters of evil: the power of the Holy Spirit. By His own choice, that power is liberated and released *only by praying people.*

The general public is convinced that brilliant and polished intellect is where the action is. We teach people to do everything but the one business that will pay the most dividends: spend time alone with God in prevailing, intercessory prayer. Prayer is striking the winning blow. Ministries are merely "gathering up the results" of prayers and praying people.

When Jesus took the challenge from His Father to change the world, He set apart twelve men. We never read that He gave them instruction in preaching, but He *did* teach them to pray.

God's deepest secrets are reserved for those who take time to "wait on Him," who take time alone with Him. He has many secrets, many spiritual visions, many hidden revelations and insights that will be shared only in the place of prayer. Satan's most successful strategy is to dilute a ministry with too much busyness (the "mechanics" of a ministry)—reading bestsellers, organizing campaigns, studying the most current methods of church growth, keeping so busy with visitation, social service and counseling that the devotional life of the church is starved and the minister becomes anemic.

For eleven years we lived in the Dakotas where we had two seasons: July and winter. I had lots of time to pray since there was snow on the ground for eight months some winters. I was shut in with God, my Bible, my typewriter and I got lots of exhorting and praying accomplished.

Now I live on the Gulf Coast of Florida and once again I have two seasons: Christmas and summer! The beach calls me to the outdoors. The seagulls and pelicans beckon. Now, probably the most complicated of accomplishments are simplicity and silence. It is much harder here in Florida to concentrate on my work and my praying.

There is no substitute for waiting on God. In prayer, we must be aware of any supposed shortcut, like going to the window at a fast food restaurant rather than waiting on God for His fullness. Be patient until you get all God intended you to have. Waiting on God brings us to our journey's end more quickly than our feet can. Or, as Charles Spurgeon said, "A man who can wait on God in prayer, can do anything." I knew this as a child, but as an adult when responsibilities press in, God has to renew it and review it in my busy mind. My memory is short.

Sometimes He brings to mind the examples of "pros." Perhaps next to Jesus, Daniel has taught me the most about prayer. I have learned from him the importance of developing prayer as a habit. Daniel prayed three times a day. Can you imagine what we could do through prayer if we were as serious about our praying as we are about eating three square meals each day? Want to change your life? To help change the world? I believe with the dedication to praying that we have to eating, we could work miracles and write history.

Daniel not only prayed, he listened. It is no small wonder that almighty God could trust Daniel with such insight concerning things to come: God's majesty; Jesus Christ being given all authority; glory and power at the end of all things. Daniel wrote the foreshadowing of what would later become the book of Revelation.

When a prayer leaves your lips, it bores immediately through the first heaven where birds and airplanes fly; it burns like a laser through the second heaven, that frozen atmosphere in the galaxy where the moon and stars are. Most Bible students believe that this is the dark atmosphere of demonic spirits inhabited by Lucifer and one-third of the angels who fell from heaven with him when he was dismissed from the presence of God. They will linger there trying to hinder prayers, and warring until the end. But your prayer, like a laser weapon, penetrates this atmosphere so rapidly it cannot be hindered. Your petition whether spoken or wished with a pure heart arrives safely in that awesome golden throne room in the third heaven where prayers are really answered!

How long does it take for a prayer to be answered? Sometimes God says wait. But sometimes, as with Daniel, He may send an angel to stand by our side with the answer (see Daniel 9:20–21). "The Lord will hear when I call to Him" (Psalm 4:3). God said through the prophet Isaiah, "Before they call, I will answer; and while they are still speaking, I will hear" (65:24). That's rapid. This happened again with Daniel in the lions' den. Before Daniel hit the floor of the den one or more angels came down and shut the lions' mouths (Daniel 6:22). He was unharmed.

Do you see how much of what happens in a person's life is determined by his prayer life? Look at this contrast. Because Daniel prayed, big hungry lions refused to attack him.

Wicked King Herod, on the other hand, refused to pray to God. He killed James and imprisoned Peter. Even though Herod witnessed the fact that Peter was rescued from prison by angels in response to prayer, he remained stiff-necked till he died (Acts 12:2–3, 11). One day while making a royal oration in his royal robe, "immediately an angel of the Lord struck him. . . . And he was eaten by worms and died" (Acts 12:23).

Compare the two men: Daniel, the young, praying man, does not die. Large lions refuse to eat him. Herod Agrippa I, a ruling king, refuses to pray and small worms eat him. It pays to pray!

How should we pray? Pray, "Father, in the name of Jesus, Your Son. . . ." When you say *Jesus* you have an immediate audience with the Almighty. He leans over the balcony of the Celestial City in response to your cry when you mention His Son. Prayers are not just words uttered in frustration to relieve psychological fears; they are powerful "energy rays" that ascend from your heart to the threshold of the golden throne room where Jesus is at the right of the Father as your personal representative. God the Father is on the throne, and all the treasures of heaven are at His disposal. Over the throne room is an awesome, emerald-colored rainbow, in a half-circle, surrounding millions of angels awaiting assignment (see Revelation 4:3).

When you pray one of three things will happen. God may dispatch strength to you, to answer your own prayer; He may send another person along to bring your answer; or, if necessary, He will send *angels* to answer your prayer. But answer He will. If not immediately, then in His time.

Elijah received all three kinds of help in response to his prayers. God gave him courage to stand up to King Ahab and the 450 false prophets. God used a widow woman to sustain him, to house him and feed him when he was hungry. And when Elijah fled for his life from Jezebel, fearful, tired and depressed, God sent an angelic chef from heaven to bake him a cake on coals, bring him water and send him on his way.

I believe seriously that the reason some people do not get prayers answered is the fact that they have not properly thanked God for things He already has done for them. Here is a suggested formula: God has given us a list of the ten most wanted behaviors for us, His children. He used Moses to help Him write these Ten Commandments for us to follow if we want to please Him. Do your best to obey.

Next, make your own list of your ten most wanted prayer answers. Then before you go any further in your prayer time, come before Him with thanksgiving. We are so spoiled we can't read God's calendar. Thanksgiving comes first, then Christmas with its gaiety and fulfilled wishes.

Philippians 4:6 instructs us clearly: "With thanksgiving, let your requests be made known unto God." Then comes the time to bring your requests before His throne. Appreciation is essential to receiving further from God.

I was fascinated by the reports of information received by Voyager 2 on its way to Neptune, and found that that operation enhanced my understanding of prayer. I read an article by George Vandeman and David Smith explaining that the whispered messages NASA received from Voyager 2 had been beamed across three billion solar miles by a faint radio signal measuring only ten quadrillionths of a watt.

Enough scientific data was received to fill six thousand sets of the *Encyclopaedia Britannica*. One scientist said, ''We're breathless with wonder. Absorbing it all is like trying to get a drink from a fire hose!'' Now, month by month, the Voyager's signal has grown fainter and may already have glided into eternal darkness beyond our reach.

But think about this: Morning by morning you and I can get down on our knees and send messages to a heavenly Kingdom. And our Father will receive those messages *instantly*, and the signals will never weaken in the cable of prayer between here and there! Our God's recording angels compute our prayers faster than the speed of light, at peak efficiency 24 hours a day, picking up the faintest whisper.

Even if your prayer is fainter than the whisper of Voyager 2, the accomplishments of Voyager 2 pale when compared to the power of prayer. One Irishman told me, ''Luck is a four-letter word spelled *p–r–a–y*.''

Prayer Warriors

Before Catherine Marshall died, she and her husband, Leonard LeSourd, established a prayer ministry, the Breakthrough Intercessors. Intercessory prayer is praying for the need of another as though it were my very own. Their Scripture theme is: ''Jesus Christ ever liveth to make intercession for us'' (Hebrew 7:25, KJV paraphrased). Prayer from this ministry of three thousand intercessors and others like it have produced remarkable results. The drastic, fast-moving changes we are seeing in Eastern Europe have largely come about through intercessory prayer.

Take the Iron Curtain. Even as in East Germany two churches had sustained prayer groups called ''the waiting room to freedom,'' the German wall between East and West came down! I know Americans with German relatives who had prayed daily for three years that

Germany would be reunited. Their praying ascended, and God has brought about this marvelous miracle of change. When I heard it on the news, I couldn't sit down. I had to stand up throughout the televised reports. God is answering prayer on a large scale, just as He has answered prayer on an individual scale as reported in previous paragraphs of this chapter.

The General Council of the Assemblies of God met in Indianapolis, Indiana, in 1989 and adopted the theme "Decade of Harvest" for the ten years to come, from 1990 up to the year 2000. What an exciting time! What do you suppose the odds are that the Iron Curtain would come crashing down coincidentally with the prayers that have been going up as the Church enters this decade of spiritual harvest?

Many married couples join together as a praying team as do any two prayer partners and stand upon this verse: "If two of you shall agree on earth as touching any thing that they shall ask, it shall be done for them of my Father which is in heaven" (Matthew 18:19, KJV).

I am impressed when two people agree on anything; that in itself is a small miracle! It is difficult for two people to pray in unity unless they write it down and pray the same prayer, believing it will happen. This is organized prayer on a small scale. It has a powerful impact.

The intercessory prayer group under the Breakthrough banner and other groups realize this concept, and know that organized, agonized, real intercessory prayer on a larger scale can move bigger mountains and affect nations.

Prayer is work. *Intercessory* prayer is laboring, advancing against the enemy. It is organized warfare. To break through enemy territory and reach the masses, it takes the masses to pray. Satan has blinded the minds of the masses. We must remember that we fight against wickedness in high places. We war not against flesh and blood, but against principalities and powers of evil. "Though we walk in the flesh [on this earth], we do not war according to the flesh. For the weapons of our warfare are not carnal but mighty in God for pulling down strongholds, casting down arguments and every high thing that exalts itself against the knowledge of God, bringing every thought into captivity to the obedience of Christ'' (2 Corinthians 10:3–5). Paul admits that he is an ordinary weak human being, but that we should not rely on ourselves; we must war in the Holy Spirit.

Just as in the military volunteers make better soldiers than reluctant draftees, so we must be diligent and *want* to be part of this militant, hell-shaking, devil-slapping, prevailing army of the invisible Kingdom.

A friend of mine met a Satan worshiper on a plane recently. In the man's hand was a list of twenty couples he was assigned to pray against, in the name of the devil. He stated, ''We have learned that if their marriage disintegrates, they become weak in their Christian faith. Next their businesses go downhill. Then the next step, their ministry falls.''

There is only one way to combat this evil force: through the blood of Jesus, as we call the invisible Kingdom to our rescue through prayer.

During the conflict we must remind ourselves, ''Greater is He who is in us than he who is in the world.'' After Jesus died on the cross, when He rose on Easter, Satan lost the war. He was cast out of heaven and defeated. Pray with confidence. Don't let the enemy intimidate you. He cannot prevent God's Kingdom from coming to earth. The only two weapons Satan has left to use on praying people are deception and bluff. Keep this in mind and take courage. The Scripture tells us that one shall chase a thousand and two will put ten thousand to flight. Two praying people are ten times as effective as one person praying alone.

When we lived in the Dakotas I was fascinated by the grain farms. There is no sight quite so beautiful as 1,200 acres of blooming sunflowers all facing the direction of the sun.

The farmers who harvest the sunflower seeds on a large scale own swathers. They are expensive pieces of machinery with a harvester arm that has a sweep 27 feet wide. This equipment costs more than the average farmer's home. But the wide sweeping effect it has during harvest is immense!

Good things are costly. God is forming a praying army. The strategy comes from heaven, but we are responsible for His battle on the earth. The equipment is expensive but the expansive effect of prevailing prayers, the sweep of reaping and harvest, will affect individuals and nations throughout eternity.

When Charles Fuller founded Fuller Seminary, he envisioned that school as a "preacher factory" to produce an army of preaching, teaching, praying soldiers to tear down the enemy's strongholds, release sin's prisoners and minister to Jesus before the Rapture. It's happening!

God is still in command on His throne. He is still in control of the nations. We are not the director. We are the extension cord for His power to minister on earth. Isaiah envisioned this when he penned, "The government will be upon His shoulder. . . . Of the increase of His government and peace there will be no end" (Isaiah 9:6–7).

Tremendous things are happening on the prophetic horizon. The Holy Spirit is being poured out. In Argentina a gray cloud of depression had settled in because of the domination of a male witch. Since people started praying, victory has come. There are 70,000 believers there now, worshiping Jesus; and the spirit of heaviness is lifting. This kind of triumph does not come from church growth seminars or through church dinners, though both of these activities are positive. Victory comes through intercessory prayer. It takes a spiritual shakeup to make things happen.

A friend of ours reports this kind of revival in China. After several dedicated people united in their praying, 3,000 were baptized on a single Sunday afternoon.

My husband has visited Russia. A year ago he started praying for that nation and he interested several Bible school students in joining him, to strengthen this prayer thrust. His heart was there. Now God is sending his body to Russia, too, along with those students for a month.

We must pray for the nations. Pray against witchcraft, pornography, economic depression and death. I think of the cliché "The more the merrier." I believe this has a spiritual application. Rallying together God's praying warriors, en masse, will bring about great victory and much personal joy for the individuals investing themselves in praying.

Jesus is coming soon, and the good news is this: It is not too late for individuals and nations to repent. God believes in honesty and justice. His judgment will prevail against sin, but His mercy is extended to those who weep in repentance, who are convicted, converted and sanctified.

The *Encyclopedia Americana* reports a most remarkable story of national intervention through the prayers of ordinary citizens. This occurred early in World War II when the British sent forces to France to join the French army and fight the German tank forces. Allied troops were defeated, however, and compressed into the third largest port city of northern France, Dunkirk. The Allied troops were 390,000 strong, but they were trapped in that bay area by the German army. If they had been annihilated or captured, Hitler would soon have launched an invasion of England and become the world ruler that he dreamed of being.

Word went out all over England: "390,000 troops trapped in the pocket at Dunkirk. Pray! Pray! Pray!" The telegraph lines clicked furiously: "Pray that God will bring the boys back to escape Hitler and the German army."

Jesus still has the government of nations upon His shoulders! The following words are printed in *Encyclopedia Americana:* "Between Dunkirk and England, the English Channel can be embroiled with wild winds and storms that make navigation impossible. By almost a miracle, the English Channel suddenly became calm as glass. While people prayed, a sudden cloud cover came and lasted from May 29 until June 2. Fishing boats, pleasure boats, any ordinary person who had any kind of a craft that would float, took off for Dunkirk. Yes, 350,000 were evacuated and made their way safely to the English shore . . . then the sky cleared.''

Troubled about the Middle East crisis? The Palestine issue? Call to God. Pray for His answer. If we would spend as much time talking to God about a situation as we talk to each other, we could move God's hand and melt hard hearts in leadership. Scripture tells us, ''In His presence is fullness of joy and at His right hand there are pleasures forevermore'' (see Psalm 16:11). But what about God's left hand? I believe the left hand of God is a warring hand, raised against the enemies of His children who pray and believe.

If you would like to join the army of praying warriors to bring healing and change to our world, I have listed below three such organized, praying groups that you might be interested in contacting. They will send you guidelines and a list of desperate needs to pray for:

Personal Needs:	*Personal and National*	*National and International*
Breakthrough	League of Prayer	Intercessors for
Catherine Marshall	P.O. Box 4038	America (IFA)
Center	Montgomery, AL	P.O. Box 2639
Lincoln, VA 22078	36104	Reston, VA 22090

Andrew Murray talked about breaking through with Christ in the school of prayer. He contended that prayer is a learned skill just as a child learns to walk or ride a bike or play the piano. By learning through practice, we learn to pray as the Holy Spirit teaches us.

Breaking Through

My husband, Carl, believes there are four ways that our prayers break through the barriers put up by the enemy and penetrate into the unseen world. Many of our projects fail because we initiate more than we can saturate with prayer. After many years in India, working with the Arabs in Egypt, in Bible schools in America and pastoring he has made some conclusions and given us some guidelines. The four ways to pray through are by the name of Jesus, dedication, the blood of Jesus and praying in the Holy Spirit. Let's look at each of these.

The Name of Jesus

In my book *Prayers that Are Answered* is a story about a little elderly lady we called "Warhorse Buckland." She was so in tune with Jesus and penetrated the unseen world with her praying so much that people said, "When she wakes up early in the morning to pray, the devil and his demons scream, 'Run! She's getting up!' " Warhorse Buckland knew the power in Jesus' name.

When Jesus spoke to His "praying Twelve" before His death, His rallying cry was that we are living on a planet targeted for attack. But He said, "I am coming back. Until then pray in My name." And He sealed that promise after His resurrection with these words: "All authority has been given to Me in heaven and on earth" (Matthew 28:18).

The disciples took that name and stood in its power and authority. In the book of Acts we read that the first of many marvelous healings took place. A lame man at the Gate Beautiful jumped up and ran into the Temple, leaping and praising God. Peter, remembering that Jesus had said His followers would perform miracles in His name, explained, "His name . . . has made this man strong" (Acts 3:16).

Later, Paul cast out demons from the possessed by the power of the name of Jesus. Certain vagabond Jews who were not believers in Jesus decided to try to use "the name without the flame." It did not work. It backfired on them.

A person must receive Christ to become a stockholder in the riches of heaven—and to speak that name with authority. By "believing on the Lord Jesus with your mind and confessing Him with your mouth'' the believer moves in realms of prayer he never dreamed of.

On the corner near our bank is a little booth containing a 24-hour night teller. You slip in your card, press your code and you can get a supply for your need. This is not unlike God's heavenly ''banking'' system. He is available 24 hours a day and the name of Jesus is the code. And as we let Him, He will pour out His supply upon us as we live a lifetime of smashing down obstacles to His Kingdom until all creation bows at the feet of Jesus.

Dedication

The second way to get through in prayer is to dedicate yourself to it. There is power in commitment. When a person is sold out to Jesus and surrendered, he has breakthrough power. ''A doubleminded man is unstable in all his ways.'' If you are ''two-faced'' and talk out of both sides of your mouth while speaking to the Almighty, your prayers will be ineffective.

Abraham became dedicated, then prayed and received the promise that he would be the father of a great nation. When you put yourself in the mode of dedication like that, you are on prayeranswered ground. Nothing is beyond the reach of prayer except that which lies outside of the will of God. ''The effective, fervent prayer [praying with fervor] of a righteous man avails much'' (James 5:16). Those who talk about prayer but don't do it are like the woman who devours romance novels but never shows real love, or the dainty lady who collects recipes but never goes into the kitchen to cook.

Spiritually impotent is the person who prays casually. Jesus deserves better than our being ''laid back.'' Whenever I hear someone say he is comfortable being laid back about prayer I think how Jesus' back suffered to answer to our petitions. Jesus is dedicated to us: ''Lo, I am with you always'' (Matthew 28:20). Are you an ''always'' person so dedicated to Him?

My dedication was tested this past week. Due to several deadlines crashing in on me at once (writing, traveling, speaking) I was exhausted when I went to Alabama as a conference speaker for the League of Prayer. I arrived feeling drained and totally without feeling or emotions.

The prayer conference was in its third day. The singing was glorious, but I sat numb. As they began to introduce me I dropped my head. I had come there on nothing but the Word, my testimony and "guts" (a crude word for dedication). Suddenly a verse came to mind out of the book of Revelation: "They overcame . . . by the blood of the Lamb and by the word of their testimony. . . . The devil has come down to you, having great wrath, because he knows that he has a short time" (Revelation 12:11–12).

Someone was asked to come forward and give a prayer. From the fourth row in the audience a large-framed man without a suit coat walked slowly but deliberately to the microphone. He gave me a slight nod and a brief smile. I had never met this man, but suddenly I knew he was a dedicated servant with an obedient spirit. He bowed his head and with a Scottish accent, his voice was deep but gentle:

"Betty, I have a word from the Lord for you. I am going to obey God. 'Thus saith the Lord: I will break the yoke of the oppressor in your life. The hand of evil has stretched out toward you, but I the Lord will smite that hand. . . . Tonight as you look within your own spirit, as you look within your own soul, you know there is no strength left in you. If the enemy comes but one more time, you will fall. You have looked outside for other strengths. All of heaven's sufficiency is yours. For the battle is not yours, but it is Mine, and I reign supreme over *all* the power of the enemy. Why should you fear and why should you be so full of care when I, your sovereign Lord, am in command? This night I will take the burden from off your shoulders, for I have taken the government and laid it on One who is mighty. I am in control, not the enemy.' Thus saith the Lord." I felt as if God had inserted a steel beam into my weak spine!

Stepping to the podium I felt the insulation of a quiet power surround me. At the close of my presentation, three men embraced Jesus as their Savior and confessed Him publicly as their Lord.

Sometimes victory in praying through comes from His name. Sometimes when there is an absence of feeling, it comes from just a determined *dedication*.

The Blood of Jesus

There is mystery in the mention of the blood of Jesus. When the powers of darkness move in, the mention of the blood changes the atmosphere. The blood of Jesus gives His followers power over our unseen enemy. The author of Hebrews talks about the blood of Jesus being shed for us in chapter 9. As the spotless Lamb, Jesus became the perfect fulfillment of the Law in His death, and mediator of a New Covenant.

When my husband, Carl, was in India, he didn't understand it, but utilized the blood of Jesus. In Thailand, he felt the powers of intense darkness, but when he stood under and preached about the blood of Jesus, and sang the old hymn "There is pow'r, pow'r, wonder-working pow'r in the blood of the Lamb" the depression lifted and the light of the world came shining through.

If you sense opposition, and cannot seem to break through, reach into the printed Word, the Bible, and read aloud the Scriptures containing the "blood" messages. You are more than a conqueror when the enemy buffets you. Reach into the resources of God. Exercise that power, your personal privilege, and He shall set you free and answer your cry.

A petite friend of mine was scheduled to give three sessions at a prayer clinic near Dickinson, North Dakota. Many people enrolled and came seeking answers to their needs. Several became frightened when they learned that in response to the ad in the paper a group of nine witches had called a "black mass" against the meeting. My little friend was aware that there were organized groups like that in San Francisco and near Boston, but in rural North Dakota?

Just before the meeting she called together three people, and simply reminded them of God's Word: "One shall chase a thousand and two will put ten thousand to flight." "There are four of us," she told them, "so we could chase twenty thousand enemies of the Lord, if necessary." She took the Bible and read aloud from the book of Exodus how the people slew a lamb and painted the lintel and doorposts with its blood. Thus the plagues of the death angel could not "cross the blood line." The women prayed together for the protective covering of the blood of the Lamb and then went in to the meeting.

At the close eighteen people knelt and wept their way into a glorious born-again experience with Jesus. His blood washed away their sinning. Nine witches against, but eighteen salvations for! We have the edge, the extra dimension of power, the blood of Jesus.

Praying in the Holy Spirit

It is the supernatural power of the Holy Spirit that comes against evil spirits with whom we are fighting. This power is released by praying in the Holy Spirit.

As Jude wrote, "But you, beloved, building yourselves up on your most holy faith, praying in the Holy Spirit, keep yourselves in the love of God" (Jude 20–21). Press on into Jesus who prays through you by the Holy Spirit *according to the will of God.*

"The Spirit also helps in our weaknesses. For we do not know what we should pray for as we ought, but the Spirit Himself makes intercession for us with groanings which cannot be uttered. Now He who searches the hearts knows what the mind of the Spirit is, because He makes intercession for the saints according to the will of God. And we know that all things work together for *good* to those who love God" (Romans 8:26–28). We are wooed by the Holy Spirit. He calls us; we are justified, then glorified through Christ. Then the Holy Spirit intercedes for us according to God's will even as Jesus intercedes for us at the right hand of God (see verses 30–35).

We read in the book of Acts that one hundred and twenty people waited in the Upper Room, according to Jesus' instructions, awaiting the Comforter, the Holy Spirit. He would be "the one called alongside to help," the *parakletos*. He would speak for Himself and pray through those in the Upper Room.

Suddenly a rushing mighty wind filled the place and they were empowered with joy and supernatural energy and began to speak in tongues as the Spirit gave them utterance, speaking languages they had not previously learned. Among the 120 was Mary, the mother of Jesus.

About sixty years ago, a group of praying, seeking people gathered together in Los Angeles, California, on Azusa Street and sought God. "Do it again!" they prayed. The Holy Spirit visited the West Coast and swept across the United States like a forest fire, saving and healing. He fell on Azusa Street then. He will fall again as believers believe.

There is no substitute for the old-fashioned formula of praying in the Spirit for supernatural, visible results. It is no small wonder young people are dropping out of church. Young people are bored with dead things; they're interested in something with energy, something lively that moves. I have visited many droopy sanctuaries. The Holy Spirit's fire would be about as welcome there as a clown at a funeral.

God is building His authentic Church, and the gates of hell shall not prevail against her. That Church in these last days will be an aggressive, praying-in-the-Spirit Church.

I know Opal Reddin from the time she was an instructor at Central Bible College in Springfield, Missouri, and I was a housemother in Flower Hall there. She wrote an article for the March 25, 1990, issue of the *Pentecostal Evangel* in which she describes this kind of praying as aggressive warfare. "The violent take [ground] by forceful praying. The greater power wins." God is infinitely greater than any power that can come against Him. There is nothing too difficult for Him (see Jeremiah 32:17). "We are *more* than conquerors through Him who loved us" (Romans 8:37).

Praying in the Holy Spirit is building yourself up in the most holy faith. Human tendency seems to dictate that when something works, make a ritual of it. We must guard against a "common" approach as to how the Spirit prays through people. The Holy Spirit is like the wind; "it bloweth where it listeth." Never take Him for granted. Keep your expression spontaneous. Variety in the Holy Spirit is essential.

Many times the Spirit leads to praise instead of petition. Praise penetrates, ascending to the throne room, touching the heart of God. Praise is the vehicle that wafts our petition heavenward. Have you ever sat down beside someone in church whose praise radiated not only upward to God, but also outward to your dry spirit and lifted you? Praise, when Spirit-wafted, penetrates. It is deliverance reaching through your circumstance, and getting hold of the invisible One, pulling Him into your realm of need. And the miracle sticks.

Effectual prayer is a key function of the Holy Spirit. To break through in prayer, sometimes you use the name of Jesus or the blood of Jesus or dedication or praying in the Holy Spirit . . . or all four.

We will never get to the place where we will know exactly how to use this gift of prayer fully. Only the Holy Spirit can do that. But as we desire to learn, we will move into deeper and deeper realms of His praying power.

5
MIRACLES FROM THE INVISIBLE

*I*f it can be explained, it is not a miracle. If it can be accomplished with ordinary human effort, it is not a miracle. Have you ever noticed how nothing is impossible to the person who doesn't have to do it himself? Well, we are going to talk about miracles that come from the unseen world. They operate on miraculous, invisible energy and we can tap into it! "For, with God, nothing shall be impossible."

The first person who heard this Scripture proclamation was the young girl Mary. The angel sent from the unseen world appeared to her, told her she would conceive a child by a miraculous implant, an act of the Holy Spirit, and bear a son. Though she was a virgin and had never known a man, it happened just that way. People today who believe this miracle are still receiving gifts, coming to them from the Source of Mary's miracle.

As poor children growing up, my four brothers and I loved Christmas—the music, the mystery of gifts hidden for us by our parents. Mother loved Christmas, too. She scrimped, worked, saved, sewed, made and bought things for us, starting sometimes in the month of June. She loved the element of surprise, and was delighted when she saw our joy on Christmas morning.

If I was good and asked her, she would occasionally give me one of my presents early. I believe God our good heavenly Father is a lot like Mother. Out of the abundance of His generous, loving heart, He sends a miracle to us here on earth early, before we get to His heaven, to let us know what heaven will be like. Much as a travel agent sends out colorful brochures to lure travelers to faraway places, God transmits an unexplainable sample that stimulates us to want to go there and to seek things that are eternal.

"And God will wipe away every tear from their eyes; there shall be no more death, nor sorrow, nor crying. There shall be no more pain, for the former things have passed away. . . . Behold, I make all things new" (Revelation 21:4–5). These words are so true. There is not a sickness on earth that heaven can't heal.

I, along with 422 other people, witnessed a miracle on earth at Leesburg, Florida, on March 3, 1990, at 8:40 P.M.

Ann Morrison, R.N., along with fourteen of her friends from Tampa, came to the Methodist Life Enrichment Center for a three-day women's retreat. Ann was diagnosed as having multiple sclerosis and a ruptured disc in her back, and was told by her doctors that she would never walk again. Ann would not accept this verdict and began speaking to any gathering that wanted to hear of her battle against an enemy that gives no comfort. Her brother, Boston Red Sox star Wade Boggs, turned her into a national symbol of hope against MS, raising large sums of money in her name to aid others similarly afflicted.

Earlier in the year, Ann had done a workshop at this same retreat center, sitting in her wheelchair, exhorting women about functioning in spite of handicap. She had read my miracle story told in the book *My Glimpse of Eternity* and told her neighbors and daughter Rachel that she was coming to the retreat to be prayed for, to receive her own miracle from God.

Ann had been in a wheelchair since September 1985. The dreaded MS attack had happened suddenly when she was 35, working fifty hours a week as a nurse practitioner, being pushed to her professional and personal limit, and loving it. Her twin daughters, Rachel and Rebecca, were juniors in high school and moving toward college and careers of their own. For the three of them, it was onward and upward. They had recovered from Ann's painful divorce and were becoming whole emotionally.

In 24 hours, it all changed. At 5:30 A.M. when the alarm clock rang, Ann swung her legs over the side of the bed and heard the cat howl. Her feet were on that cat's tail and the cat was biting her ankles angrily, but she could not feel it. She drove herself to work somehow; she could not feel the car pedals beneath her feet at all.

Terrified, she went immediately to the neurologist in her medical building. By the time they hospitalized her, both legs were totally useless. Her hands and arms were so weak she could hardly lift a fork, and her hands trembled so badly that lifting that fork brought no guarantee the food would reach her mouth.

After one month in the hospital she was diagnosed with the catastrophic disability of chronic, progressive multiple sclerosis. She continued to lose ground, even though she worked hard at her daily therapy.

Nursing was Ann's life and without the ability to reach out and help people she had a hard time telling who she was. Three months later she found something to do. From her wheelchair she spoke to discouraged groups of chronically ill and disabled persons. She talked to the groups about forgiveness. She had forgiven her husband for leaving her and for the painful divorce that had split up their family. (He was given custody of their young son.)

One of her daughters, Rachel, stayed with her over the years and lovingly and patiently helped Ann get ready for the retreat. The trip left Ann exhausted and wondering if she could even make it to the first session on Saturday. She went and enjoyed it immensely. After eating a little lunch, she was drained and asked Rachel to push her back to the room and help her to bed.

In the early afternoon, Ann asked Rachel, "Please see if Betty

Malz will come to my room so I can meet her and shake hands with a miracle."

I've asked Ann to tell the rest of the story in her own words:

Betty came into that room like an energetic tornado. She hugged me, she talked and I listened. She asked me some questions about forgiveness, then gently and persistently explored my spirit. Betty told me about Eleanor Olson in North Dakota who was healed of MS during an anointing service, after thirteen years of suffering slurred speech, blurred vision and walking only with the aid of a walker. My heart leaped. Was it possible? Could it be that I would be healed?

At this point Betty stopped and asked thoughtfully, "Are you familiar with the healing service in which they anoint with oil?" I said that I was, both from church and the hospital.

Betty asked me, "Would you be willing to participate in such an anointing service this evening?"

Would I be willing? "If my daughter has to carry me in, I will be there!" I cried loudly and eagerly.

That evening following dinner when I stood to speak, I explained to the women that I had not planned to pray for the sick, but if any woman with a habit, depression, affliction or emotional problem would come forward, we would pray for her. I explained that the night before Jesus went to the cross, He knelt on the Mount of Olives and prayed for our sins *and* our sicknesses. I talked about Isaiah 10:27: "The yoke will be destroyed because of the anointing oil." Not just anointing of joy for ministry or service, but anointing to break the yoke of our personal bondage.

Then I quoted from James 5:14: "Is anyone among you sick? Let him call for the elders of the church, and let them pray over him, anointing him with oil in the name of the Lord. And the prayer of faith will save the sick, and the Lord will raise him up. And if he has committed sins, he will be forgiven." I explained to the audience that I could do nothing, but had been instructed by the Holy Spirit just before the meeting, *Just let Jesus.* We get our roles mixed up.

We are merely the pray-ers. *He* is the healer. I instructed them to come forward and as I prayed, to speak His name, "Jesus," looking to Him, raising their hands to surrender their need to Him, reaching out, lifting their arms to receive what He would give them in exchange.

Several women who had indicated they had a need lined up quietly and passed by the eight women on the board, four on each side of me. I held a bottle of olive oil to anoint each forehead in simple, childlike faith as instructed by James. Let's hear Ann's account again.

My daughter pushed my wheelchair into the line. Rolling forward, I began silent, whispered praying. I acknowledged, *I am a sinner. I can't change that, but You, Jesus, can. I am unworthy.* Then I thanked God for sending His Son to hang on the cross and die for me, and appreciated Him for loving me. I talked to God and assured Him that if this was not my time to be healed I would not be disappointed. Now that Jesus was my Savior, I knew I would someday be healed in heaven. Five years had passed and I had nearly become reconciled to my handicap, but I vowed that if He healed me, I would serve Him and serve people the rest of my days! That was no light promise. That was my serious commitment.

For the rest of the time approaching the front of the auditorium, I just breathed the name "Jesus, Jesus." The four ladies to the left of Betty touched me lovingly, then I received Betty's anointing, her prayer. Then I rolled in my wheelchair to her right where four other loving women either shook hands with me or patted me thoughtfully. They were having faith for me, too. I began to feel sweet peace. I began to feel strength and felt incredibly whole and unexplainably serene.

When I prayed for Ann, I heard a man's voice in my inner spirit, *Tell her to stand up and walk.* I argued with this impulse, thinking in the negative, the natural, *Malpractice.* I prayed silently, "Lord, let her walk." Then as I went to pray for a lady who wanted deliverance from smoking . . .

I heard a man's voice. It was not Betty! This was a women's retreat but it was a man's voice and it said, *Stand up and walk.* It was the voice of my Lord! I stopped the wheelchair, put my feet down and looking at Rachel said, "I'm going to walk back to our seats!" *I did!*

Now, I had not walked for five years because of MS and for a year had been dealing with a ruptured disc in my back so that I could not sit up. It had been so painful to move around. But I stood up. My legs did not shake, my step was firm and I walked back to our seats. The next thing I did was get down on my knees to the Lord and thank Him, for I had not knelt for five years. It felt wonderful, wonderful! I bent and there was absolutely no pain in my back when I touched my toes.

Before my mother died in 1986 she told me I would be healed. I am sure the Lord let her know so that she could rejoice with us that night at my healing.

Just two weeks after Ann's healing miracle, she rented a car and drove to Tallahassee to help Rebecca move. She then drove to Gainesville to show her father what had happened.

Thanksgiving Day, November 22, 1990, the front page of the *Tampa Tribune* carried the story in full color:

"Every day is Thanksgiving Day now! As Hamlet basically said to Horatio, 'More things happen in this world than you have the philosophy to explain.' " There were several photographs. One showed Ann's brother pushing her in her wheelchair at the 1989 celebrity softball game in St. Petersburg. Alongside was a photo of Ann rushing up to hug her brother this year at Al Lang Stadium. She needed no help.

Tampa Tribune staff writer Joe Henderson told me, "Betty, I have known Ann Morrison a long time. She was my doctor's nurse. I knew she had been in a wheelchair for five years, and when I saw her running up and down the bleachers, laughing and socializing with fans, I nearly collapsed with shock. I knew I had to have her story. Good news should always be front page news!"

Thinking back just several weeks ago to Ann's healing, I am

amazed at the stillness of so great and powerful a miracle. I remember Jesus' words when He said, "Stand still, and see the salvation of the Lord." I have attended sensational, noisy, hyped meetings in a crowd of people who were high on an event, instead of being high on Jesus, and nothing happened.

When we women prayed for Ann, we stood on quiet power, silently watching Him work! When we have seen the miraculous workings of God in some other marvelous cases of healing and providential deliverance, the thing that has impressed us most has been the quietness with which it has all been done, the absence of everything spectacular and sensational, and the utter sense of humility that came to us as we stood in the presence of this mighty God. We felt how easy it was for Him to do it all without the faintest effort on His part or the slightest help on ours!

Now that Ann had recovered miraculously from MS, she went to see her doctor to schedule the surgery he had recommended to repair the ruptured disc. He found nothing wrong with either her back or her legs. No surgery was necessary!

God the Creator and His Son, Jesus, through the power of the Holy Spirit, this triune God is our unseen Source in making miracles come down from heaven to earth! I believe many miss the miracle because they seek only miracles or a ministry or spend time poking at the devil instead of just seeking Jesus.

A.B. Simpson, founder of the Christian and Missionary Alliance, put it this way:

> Once His gifts I wanted, now the Giver own.
> Once I sought for healing, now Himself alone.

Miracles are rarely singular. Recently Carl asked Ann to come to our church and tell her story. At the close of the service, we were amazed that she stood for more than thirty minutes with my husband and me while we prayed for the needs of people.

One young woman who had ulcers since college was healed *before* she was prayed for. She is eating everything she wants now.

One man with chronic high blood pressure we had prayed for found out the following day that his blood pressure was normal. (He had it checked at the local hospital.)

An older couple stepped forward to speak to Ann, and we prayed for them both. He had suffered a stroke and his entire right side was immobile. He was swinging his right arm and declaring, "It's alive again!" His wife had struggled just to get from the car into the church, and now she is walking and riding her bike through the mobile home park where they live, two miles per day.

David the psalmist received a miracle from the unseen world, too. His was not healing, but help to do battle for the armies of God against the enemies of the Lord. David was not a big shot with a slingshot. He learned to aim rocks at animals that might harm the sheep while an apprentice shepherd watching his family's flocks. He probably learned to use a slingshot with great accuracy while just a little boy. In fact, he was still just a boy with no military training of war strategy when he faced the giant Goliath and the entire Philistine national army.

David said, "My help comes from the Lord. The Lord is my rock." When he used what he had, what he knew, willing to risk it for God, then the unique and powerful unseen factor came from the unseen world to make up the difference. I believe that the supernatural force and deadly accuracy of that small rock was directed either by a wind from heaven or an unseen angel with great strength to the small vulnerable area on the giant's forehead, and the ninefoot Goliath fell to the ground dead.

This was a true miracle from the Lord. Probably a greater miracle was the fact that the military men were willing to let David try. All he had was "God and a rock." That's pretty elementary ammunition. But if it works, don't fix it. These were the two things he tried and trusted—his seen slingshot and his unseen God.

My friend Karen Siddle was strolling barefoot along Clearwater Beach when her left big toe struck a rock. Stooping, she picked it up and dried it with her beach towel. Later, with a magic marker, she wrote on one side "Betty" and on the other side "Giant Killer."

I carry it in my purse or briefcase as my constant reminder that all I will ever need to kill any giants that loom up in my life is "God and a rock." He *is* my rock.

I mentioned the virgin Mary earlier and would like to draw our attention to her once more. Like David, she was also very young when she received a miracle—the miracle of miracles—from the unseen world. Perhaps there is a key here as to how we can receive miraculous intervention: have simplistic, childlike faith, believing in the Source though we cannot see the answer and though it may never have happened before.

God recognized what Mary did have: purity and humility. Because of her gentle, willing spirit, the Holy Spirit touched her and enabled her to conceive the Lord Jesus, Son of the living God. She did not question anything, but believed the angel Gabriel when he brought her the personal telegram from the unseen world. "The Holy Spirit will come upon you, and the power of the Highest will overshadow you; therefore, also, that Holy One who is to be born will be called the Son of God. . . . For with God nothing will be impossible" (Luke 1:35, 37).

Later we read that Mary kept all the marvelous praises of her Son and pondered them in her heart. (Luke 2:19). Thus we see other qualities—quiet confidence and the ability to keep a secret. Mary was wiser than her young years. I am sure you know some women who, had this happened to them, would have been on network television proclaiming it. I believe we would see more of the glory of God and the miraculous if God found more people who could keep a confidence.

Since Jesus' birth was not possible from a human standpoint, we need not expect that anything that He chooses to do for us from the invisible Kingdom has to be "possible" either. We need to think on a new level of possibility.

You may wonder many times where God is, but He always knows where you are. You have access to His help and protection if you will but ask. According to the Bible, there are millions of angels available to help on command—ten thousand times ten thousand.

According to a recent poll, if only twenty percent of the religious people who do believe in angelic help from the invisible Kingdom are utilizing this power, then there is a great excess of angelic assistance available to those who do tap that great source of help. As James said, "Ye have not, because ye ask not" (James 4:2, KJV). I believe a man or woman whose head and knees are bent in believing prayer can go by faith where armies would fear to go, places where he or she could never afford to be.

We sing a chorus at church about reaching out to touch the Lord. If you recall, this is exactly what a woman in the Bible did. She had an issue of blood for twelve years. She had spent all her money on physicians who could not help her. She had only grown worse. She learned that Jesus was coming through her town, and said out of desperation, "If I could but touch Him, I could be whole." She made her way through the crowds, reached out and just touched the fringe of His robe. That was a feeble, weak but powerful reach for Jesus, who affirmed her and healed her (Matthew 9:20–22).

A man in another crowd reached forth his withered hand and it was restored, made whole like his other hand (Matthew 12:13).

Probably even a greater miracle was when Zacchaeus, a tax collector of small stature, climbed a tree and "went out on a limb" for the Lord (see Luke 19). He merely climbed up and looked at Jesus, didn't touch Him physically, but touched His heart just the same. Jesus called him by name and went to eat with the man who had been cheating people out of their funds. Jesus made him into an honest person who paid back all he took by false pretense.

For a small investment of "reaching" in childlike faith, what great dividends are sent directly from the throne room of God to us here.

Lawrence Bloxsom of Pinellas Park, Florida, learned the lesson of reaching out through his great need. One day he found himself in an impossible situation when his earthly resources had failed him. He was desperate.

Lawrence stood by the hospital bed of his suffering wife, tormented by her pain. Her cancer had spread from a breast into a lung, and then into the bone marrow. Extensive radiation, chemotherapy, medications and surgery to remove part of her lung had been tried but all attempts seemed downhill steps to death.

The continual medical bills were daily reminders of her plight and made Lawrence dread opening the mailbox. The bills arrived like confetti from doctors he had never heard of. *Difficult* is a mild word to describe the hours spent in hospital waiting rooms and for the results of medical tests to determine what action would be taken next.

Medical science was trying everything possible, but it was obviously not enough. Frantic, he reached into his earliest childhood memories and recalled his father talking about "laying on of hands" and asking Jesus to heal the sick. He was ignorant about the procedure, and his wife had never heard of such a thing. They had never discussed spiritual matters in their thirty years of marriage. They did not believe reports of miraculous power from God.

But when he told his wife he was going to "try to reach God" for help, to his absolute amazement she grabbed his hand and thrust it over her incision and said, "Pray."

Fear welled up in Lawrence's mind and he tried to withdraw his hand. He was 57 years old and had never prayed for anyone. He had thought "faith" people had to be brainwashed to do this. But something occurred that was beyond his ability to explain. He said, "Remove this pain." His wife continued to moan with pain. He tried again. This time he began with, "Father, remove my wife's pain." Then, to his amazement, he recalled a Scripture from somewhere in his Sunday school days: "When a son asks a father for bread, He will not give him a stone."

In response to his attempt at praying, he felt God come into the room and heard His voice. Lawrence told me, "I shall never forget the sound of that voice. It came from over my head and sounded younger than my own voice."

He went on to tell me, "Though I had never heard or talked to God before, He knew my voice and I knew His!" God told him, "It will be done."

"His was the voice of a kingly Lord and a Father to be worshiped and praised in all circumstances. It blended into a regal voice of the King of kings and was a factual power that whatever He said was completed as He said it. How strange that I learned so very much in just a moment's time."

Lawrence went on, "A mere phrase or sentence could have created a thousand new words, effortlessly. Had my mind been capable of comprehending the dimensions of infinity, there would have been no spoken reply. I was awestruck. Here was all the power of the universe. I had just heard the voice of my Shepherd. A supreme authority, spoken in love and humility. I only heard a sentence, but it was enough that I knew that God's plans when made will be carried out. There is much more going on in the spirit world than we can see or imagine."

Almost immediately his wife fell into a restful sleep. The following morning when she awakened the chest pain was gone. The incision was no longer infected and raw, but appeared like a scar from an incision ten months before. She has not had a chest pain since.

The Great Physician had passed through the room and kept His word and healed her.

God's ways are unfathomable. Some four hundred women were on hand to witness Ann Morrison's miracle after years of prayers that seemingly had no effect. Lawrence Bloxsom, on the other hand, received a miracle for his wife at the first attempt. However He gives them, miracles are God's gift, free samples of the world to come dropped down, unearned, unmerited, wrapped in His mercy and loving grace.

6
INVISIBLE PROTECTION

H ow do angels make contact with us? Few people have seen those important "helpers" from heaven. We can't reach out and touch them just because we want to, but they can touch us when it becomes necessary. Angels are dispatched in emergencies when we pray to Jesus and when human help is not available. Sometimes they instruct, coach, fight for, guard and tend to the safety of God's children. Angels are capable of physically helping, protecting or guiding people through desperate circumstances. Having angelic help is just one of the fringe benefits of the believer.

Angels are created beings, not spirits of dead, departed loved ones. Though they are spirits, they ofttimes have appeared in visible, even human form. In *Angels Watching Over Me*, I told the Jennifer Church story. She was born with a brain tumor that enlarged and threatened her life. I mention it here because it is one of the stories that people have written me about the most. Since angels come and go, they ask, do the miracles really hold?

You may remember that little Jennifer was scheduled for surgery to have the tumor removed. Her parents were sitting on the porch of their home in Wellington, Kansas, when a shabbily dressed elderly man, walking very slowly, came up their front sidewalk, stepped onto the porch and requested something to eat. Jennifer's mother went to the kitchen and brought back a sandwich and a glass of milk. She set it on the small table near the elderly man. Without even looking at the food or saying a word, he opened the screen door, entered the house uninvited and proceeded down the hallway toward the sick child's room.

The parents watched with disbelief as the old man reached into the crib, picked up the baby and placed her gently against his chest! Jennifer had always been terrified of strangers and especially of late since the tumor had enlarged and she suffered so with pain in her head.

The old man's voice whispered softly with authority and peaceful assurance: "You will be all right. You will not need surgery." He held her close for a moment, placed a nickel in her small fist, put her back in her crib and suddenly just disappeared from sight.

The following day at Kansas City Children's Hospital after hours of examinations, Jennifer was dismissed, sent home, no surgery necessary. The family has always felt that one of Jesus' healing angels disguised as an old man ministered this unexplainable miracle.

Since moving back to Florida, I had lost contact with this family. But there in this morning's mail was a wedding announcement. Little Jennifer Church is now a grown, healthy, lovely young woman soon to be married. Yes, the miracle still holds.

Many times angels come to the aid of the person praying; other times they assist the person being prayed for. Angels guide the believer and are interested in conversions. They are glorious beings with great knowledge ministering to those who are to become heirs of salvation (see Hebrews 1:14).

I met Robert's parents at the Honeywell plant south of Clearwater, Florida. They had read the Jennifer Church story and wanted to share what happened with their wayward son.

One night Robert's father sat reading his Bible. Suddenly both he and his wife felt alarm for their son. They prayed for him regularly to make a serious commitment with his life, but this was different. There was no explainable reason for their concern for Robert's safety, but the force that fell upon them was unquestionably a communication from the Holy Spirit.

Robert's father dropped to his knees, Bible still in hand, and prayed aloud to almighty God who can change or suspend all forces in the universe. "Lord, invade Robert's predicament. If necessary, send angels to warn him or protect him." They could not reach Robert by phone but three days later they received a letter from him describing an accident that had occurred 2,000 miles away in the state of Illinois at the exact time that his father had prayed for him.

Dear Dad and Mother,

My two friends and I were riding our motorcycles down a dark country road at night. A race started and we were doing in excess of eighty miles per hour. I zoomed past the others and took the lead. Suddenly I came up on an unlighted, radical turn. My first realization of the turn came when I was flying into the darkness of a wooded area. I tried to jump but my cycle struck something and bucked me like a wild mule. That's the last thing I remember.

I do not know how long I lay on my stomach. The cycle was on its side in two pieces. I regained consciousness and had no idea how three police cars were already on the scene. I must have been in shock longer than I realized. They rolled me over easy, sure that my body would be broken badly. I had missed a steel telephone support wire, an open concrete wall and several trees. I was taken to the hospital and released.

The following day, returning to the scene, I found my glasses two hundred feet beyond where my body had come to rest. Something or someone had placed them carefully on a bush nearby. They were hanging there on that bush unbroken. Seems as if a courier with a great sense of humor had sent me a message that my running was over, and that time was running out for me. I was badly shaken, but unhurt; not even a scratch. I am now listening.

As Robert put it later, "My heavenly Father spoke to my earthly father, warned him and rewarded his praying. My earthly father's prayer bore upward into the heavenlies and though he prayed 2,000 miles from the scene, help was there when I first skidded. It was obvious to me that both my parents loved me a lot. I realized that in spite of my shortcomings and failures, I was safe when I could have been paralyzed or dead. I made an about-face in my life."

It seems that an angel did a double assignment of courier messenger to the parents and protector of the son they had prayed for so long.

I believe we receive invisible protection more times than we are aware of. I already mentioned that our daughter April has been living alone in a small motel, just blocks from the scene of those hideous campus murders in Gainesville, Florida. We have been concerned for her safety, especially since the victims of those murders fit her description (college-aged girls living just off campus).

We all wrestled with the idea of her just quitting her job, pulling out of that dangerous location and coming home. She is not a quitter and needs the money to attend Emory University next semester. So she stayed.

Early one morning after a long session of talking to God, in which I asked Him to send either visible or invisible protection to her, Scriptures began rolling across my mind's screen, almost like the tiny screen of my computer. They came so hard and fast I could barely write them down. But I did write them down, and mailed them immediately to April. I felt I had sent her an insurance policy, and peace descended on both her and us, her parents. She was kept safely. Below is that list of promises.

"Your life is hid with Christ in God" (Colossians 3:3, KJV). If her life was hidden, then no murderer could find her.

"In the shadow of Your wings I will make my refuge, until these calamities have passed by" (Psalm 57:1).

"Let the angel of the Lord chase them [who plot your hurt]" (Psalm 35:5). (The angel of the Lord will fight for you!)

"God is our refuge and strength, a very *present* help in trouble" (Psalm 46:1).

"Whenever I am afraid, I will trust in You" (Psalm 56:3).

"I will both lie down in peace, and sleep; for You alone, O Lord, make me dwell in safety" (Psalm 4:8).

April kept a copy of these under her pillow at night and hidden in her clothing during those crucial days and weeks . . . and was safe!

Angels also help us in regard to the elements—wind, fire, storms and pestilence. I personally believe, for instance, that there is a special sailor's angel.

I like to think Paul believed this, too. In Acts 27 we read that he was prisoner on board a ship sailing toward Italy. Sailing was bad and when they came to a place named Fair Havens on Crete, Paul warned them to stay. The centurion would not listen to Paul and put out to sea. Not long after that, a tempestuous wind caught the ship. They took shelter off the island Clauda, repaired the ship and fled the quicksands. The sun was hidden by dark, overcast, stormy skies and they were without light for many days. Both crew and prisoners gave up hope of survival.

Paul held his peace for a while, then said, "Men, you should have listened to me, and not have sailed from Crete and incurred this disaster and loss. And now I urge you to take heart, for there will be no loss of life among you, but only of the ship. For there stood by me this night an angel of the God to whom I belong and whom I serve, saying, 'Do not be afraid, Paul; . . . God has granted you all those who sail with you.' Therefore take heart, men, for I believe God that it will be just as it was told me" (Acts 27:21–25).

A number of days later the ship went aground and broke into pieces. Some swam, some floated on broken boards, but all 276 passengers arrived safely on shore.

Most of my life, our family has had a sizable boat and I have always remembered the story of Paul and the angel. Before my first husband, John, died, he was always a careful boatman and prayed before launching our craft into the Gulf of Mexico near our home. There is a lovely spot just offshore where the sunsets can range from pale pink to brilliant golden orange. At sundown many commercial fishermen, shrimpers and novice fishermen with cane poles turn off their engines to view God's artistic beauty and to hear the chimes each evening coming from the Community Church on shore.

John died when our daughter, Brenda, was twelve. Four months after his death, our second baby, April, was born. One morning looking out the family room window at breakfast, Brenda glanced over at me and said, "Mother, I miss Daddy, and I miss taking the boat out every Tuesday, like we did when he was here." John had named our small cabin cruiser the *Betty Lynn*, for me and for Brenda Lynn.

I called my brothers that morning and my dad, but they were all too busy to go with us and help with the boat. We decided to go alone. Launching at the Dunedin marina, we were pleasantly surprised that we did not have to wait; ours was the only boat there.

We strapped the five-month-old baby into her jump seat, put her safely in the cabin and took off toward Honeymoon Island. It brought back memories of my husband fishing for flounder. Probably a half-mile off Hurricane Pass, I dropped anchor and we ate an early lunch out of the sack. We ate rather hurriedly because the wind seemed to be coming up and the sky was overcast with a strange pale green color.

Suddenly it happened—a boater's nightmare. The wind shifted and gusts sent waves over our rocking boat. The valleys between swells were deeper than the *Betty Lynn*. The clouds dumped walls of water at strange and adverse angles again and again across the hull. I could not see. While I tried to steer toward what I thought might be the direction of shore, Brenda stood by me with a towel wiping my glasses, first one lens, then the other. I was thankful for one thing: The baby did not cry.

We prayed; oh, did we pray! "O God, send us help. Help us to find the shore." I believe God puts on an extra crew of guardian angels for children, old people and, speaking personally, stupid young widows.

The lightning frightened us especially. It seemed to flash around us like boomerangs. During one bolt of lightning and clap of thunder, I saw a tiny, faint light in front of us. We followed it with great difficulty to shore. I had no idea I would even be strong enough to steer us in.

When we were finally pulled into the dock and tied securely, I tried to tease several men on the dock. "Which one of you is the sailor's angel?" None of them smiled. They pointed out one angry man from the Coast Guard shore patrol who had apparently been calling me some awful names for taking a boat out when they had been issuing small-craft warnings since 7:00 A.M. We had not heard the news or turned on the radio.

None of us ever figured out what the tiny light was that led us safely to shore. I learned the importance of safety precautions from this lesson, but also found my belief in invisible protection reaffirmed. Scripture tells us that "He shall give His angels charge over you, to keep you in all your ways"—waterways, airways, walkways and roadways.

It is possible for angels to be invisible to some while visible to others. Paul Hamelink has been a friend of our family for several years. He worked with my husband at Trinity College. His Grandma Hamelink experienced invisible escort protection.

She had survived the brutal Boer War in South Africa, and came as an immigrant to America from the Netherlands. Arriving in Kenosha, Wisconsin, in 1910 as a lanky twenty-year-old, she found great comfort in attending one of the early Pentecostal assemblies. Walking to church in daylight was a joy, even though she went through some bad neighborhoods. But coming home well after dark was frightening.

One particular night the thing she had always feared would happen did happen. Rowdy, drunken men rounded the corner and were coming toward her. She only had time to pray quickly, "God, send protection." The men stopped suddenly, as if startled by what they saw. Then they jumped sideways, clear off the sidewalk, giving her an extra-wide berth as though there were two or more people walking beside her.

After that episode, she was no longer afraid to walk to church, and has always believed that her angelic escort, unseen to her, was seen by her "would-have-been" attackers.

I have always thought of angels without sexual distinction, or else visualized them as strong male warriors. Recently, I found a couple of lady angels in the Bible. Zechariah 5:9 says, "Then I raised my eyes and looked, and there were two women, coming with the wind in their wings; for they had wings like the wings of a stork, and they lifted up the basket between earth and heaven."

Angels can read and write. Much is said in Scripture about "recording" angels. The book of Revelation repeats more than once, "Unto the angel . . . write. . . ." God also speaks through angels. They act as signposts to point us in the proper direction, not to interfere with our spiritual balance. The unseen spiritual world is a reality. It is the coming, ultimate reality. It has always been in existence and will remain throughout eternity.

Angels not only assist individuals, but tend to the affairs of nations. In 2 Kings 18 and 19, we read that Sennacherib, king of Assyria, the enemy of the living God, came against King Hezekiah. When Hezekiah received a letter from the battlefront and read it, he went to the house of the Lord and spread the letter out before the Lord. I am glad our God is not an image made of gold, wood or stone, but is a God who could read that letter. Then Hezekiah prayed that the Lord God of Israel would see them through the battle.

Soon thereafter the angel of the Lord went out and smote 185,000 enemies. When God's children got up the next morning they found 185,000 corpses lying on the ground.

The enemy king Sennacherib ran and stopped at Ninevah to worship and try to appease his false god, and while he was doing that, his own two sons Adrammelech and Sharezer killed him with their own swords.

Angels will defend, protect and deliver God's servants. (See also Daniel 6:22; Acts 5:19; 12:8–11; and 27:23–24.)

A few short years ago, Dr. Louise D'Oliveira left England and flew to Nairobi, Kenya, where she has worked nonstop as one of the top literacy engineers in the world. For her trip across Africa teaching the underprivileged to read and write, and telling of the love of God, she purchased a secondhand Volkswagen Beetle for $600.

Driving alone on the trip she remembered a newspaper story the week before about two men, not in a VW but in a truck, who had stopped at a railroad crossing in that same area and had been suddenly attacked by one rogue elephant. With his huge body, he smashed the truck time after time, rolling it over and over.

During Louise's long trip teaching literacy classes she had an attack of malaria three times, was heartbroken over the hunger of the people and encountered herds of elephants several times that nearly caused her heart to stop beating. After teaching some seven hundred literacy classes, she was heading back to Nairobi, exhausted. Late in the day she took her little Volkswagen off the main road onto a dirt trail toward the Mweya Lodge on Lake George to spend the night. Suddenly dark forms loomed up in the distance. Elephants . . . six of them! They were full-grown and right in the middle of the road, giving each other dust baths. She stopped, turned off the engine and waited and prayed. The nearest shelter was seventeen miles ahead. She could not go back: She had passed three elephants near the road not too far back and the bull elephant had challenged her.

While she waited, trying to decide what to do, the sun set. There on the hill ahead they started moving toward her; she counted seventeen at first and more were coming over the horizon. She had stumbled upon a whole herd, and the one king elephant, the lead bull, was larger than any living creature she had ever seen.

She prayed, "O Lord, I know how to get across a busy street in a city, but I cannot get out of a herd of wild elephants, out here all alone. I am considered their intruder and I have frightened them with my car. I am helpless. Please help me."

Fear clutched her, paralyzing her movement and thought. She could not sit there and wait for death, yet if she started the engine and startled them, they would panic.

She took the chance. She started the engine and pressed hard on the accelerator. The little car shot forward. Several elephants turned into the road just in front, but she scooted past them safely with inches to spare on each side. Just ahead turning a bend in the road she encountered a sight that brought chills. Elephants were not only on each side, they were in the middle of the road. She was caught.

Looking into the rearview mirror she saw a dark wall moving up behind her, chasing her—trunks up, ears out and dust flying. Leading the charge was a creature so mammoth that the tops of his legs were even with the top of her car! She had only one choice: to move forward fast. She could feel the pounding, jarring steps of the irate herd moving up behind her, seconds away. She prayed, "Sweet Jesus, make an opening large enough for my car to pass through. Send angels to scatter them."

One elephant on the road ahead of her moved, made a narrow opening in that massive gray wall of beasts. . . . Was it enough? She accelerated forward and elephants shifted on either side. She did not look up, but drove so fast that the hair on her head was flying straight out! Another burst of speed and she was ahead of them. As she drove the miles toward Mweya Lodge she knew that an angel of the Lord had directed traffic and made a VW-sized hole just for her.

As she arrived at the lodge, fatigue and shock set in, but she bowed her head and let pass over her again and again the calm that comes from the "cradle of safety" in Jesus.

Here are affirmations about angels that are a source of help and comfort to me:

- The good angels are spectators while the Church engages in fierce battle with the hosts of sin (see 1 Corinthians 4:9). This is an incentive to endurance.

- They escort the dead heavenward (Luke 16:22).

- They gather the elect at the end of all things (Matthew 24:31).

- They guard the bodies of the elect dead just as Michael guarded Moses' body (Jude 9) and two angels guarded Christ's tomb (Luke 24:4).

- They will accompany Christ at His Second Coming and separate the righteous from the wicked (Matthew 25:31; 13:39–42; 2 Thessalonians 1:7–10).

- They are innumerable (Hebrews 12:22).

- They are mighty in power, though not almighty (2 Thessalonians 1:7).

- They are beings of great power, but their power is delegated (Revelation 22:16).

- They excel in strength. It took only one to destroy 185,000 Assyrians in one night (2 Kings 19:35).

- Many times they carry out justice, policing territories. Two angels destroyed Sodom and Gomorrah (Genesis 19:1).

- One angel is all that will be needed to bind Satan and cast him into the bottomless pit (Revelation 20:1–3).

- They stand on the four corners of the earth (Revelation 7:1).

- The archangels Michael and Gabriel are among the principalities and powers of the spirit world as great leaders (Daniel 10:13; Luke 1:19).

- The angels have a ministry of priestly service and worship in heaven (Revelation 5:11–12; 8:3–4).

- Their earthly ministry touches the affairs in the material sense, too (showing Hagar a fountain, appearing before Joshua with a drawn sword, releasing Peter's chains, opening prison doors, feeding, strengthening and defending).

- And with all these other jobs angels have, the Lord will give His angels charge concerning *you* (Matthew 4:6)!

7

INVISIBLE POWER
(GOD'S YELLOW PAGES)

*T*his help from the unseen world is available upon request. The Father in heaven will give the Holy Spirit to those who ask Him (Luke 11:13). And the last thing Jesus said at His ascension just before He raised His hands and was translated back to heaven was: "Behold, I send the Promise of My Father upon you; but tarry . . . until you are endued with power from on high" (Luke 24:49).

At the age of thirteen I embraced Jesus as my personal Savior while kneeling at a brown, floral print couch in our rural Indiana home, between my mother and father who prayed with me. I slept that night with sweet peace that my passport visa for the world to come was in order. I came to understand that Christ lived within me now by the power of the Holy Spirit.

At the age of sixteen, my faith began to waver. I needed something more. I wanted to be liked, to be popular and would dress fancily, laugh loudly or play jazz piano rapidly to be "in" and accepted. Since the age of eight, I had dreamed of being a writer, but the books that were popular were not the kind that a pastor's daughter could write. This restlessness, this invisible negative pull at my emotions, these temptations—what was the source? How could I combat them? Where could I find a cure?

I went to my mother. She was one of the happiest, most well-adjusted women I knew. A pastor's wife with five lively children, she was overwhelmed with activities and demands. She could not take much time, but told me that when she was my age, she faced the same dilemma. She searched through Scripture and learned about the "gift" of the Holy Ghost, an empowerment from Him, a "second blessing" as John Wesley had called his own experience of the infilling of the Holy Ghost. She said she learned that this Comforter was the One called alongside to help, to fight life's battles for her. She told me I could find out about this unusual dimension for living in the Gospel of John and Acts.

Entranced, I went to my quiet grandmother, Mom Burns. "Do you know about this?" I inquired.

"Oh, yes," she whispered. "Most people don't know, but this quiet power is what sustains me."

Next I sought out my paternal grandmother, Mom Perky, a tall, outgoing Englishwoman, so full of self-confidence she seemingly was never afraid of people, life or the devil. I rode my bicycle across the road to her house. While we ate some of her homemade date-stuffed cookies, she told me frankly, "What you need is to wait until you are endued with power from on high. You will receive power to resist the enemy of your soul after the Holy Spirit comes."

When she went to the oven to take out another pan of hot cookies, I did some quick, serious thinking. If I was born to be a writer, maybe the devil was trying to keep me weak or cause me to fail so that my dream would not come true. Jesus is a dream-maker; Satan is a dream-breaker. I didn't know it then, but maybe the enemy of my soul already knew that I would write books showing the way to Jesus, salvation and the unseen world. The devil had schemed to prevent me from receiving the assistance to do it.

Returning to the table, Mom Perky explained to me that God was the Source of this power. Jesus came to earth to introduce Him, this third Person of the Trinity, and the Holy Spirit was the conduit or power line or lifeline between the unseen world and the earth. We could plug into this power by asking. I determined to get this extra help, and began my search.

I was so thirsty for that Source of power and was so deep into the Bible that following Friday evening that I missed the basketball game at Otter Creek High School. I never missed a basketball game for I was dating Ron, the high-point man on our team my junior year. Yet I was close to finding some answers and couldn't quit. In Acts 1:13–14 were listed the names of some of the "greats" who were in the Upper Room and who had received this empowerment. Among others were Peter, John, James, Andrew, Philip, Thomas, Matthew and Mary, the mother of Jesus! That did it! If it was good enough for the virgin Mary, it was good enough for me. If a pure woman like her needed this experience, for sure I needed it. I wanted it more than I wanted food.

Reading on I learned that receiving the Holy Spirit was not a one-shot experience of religious adrenaline. In John 14 and 15, I read that the Holy Spirit would descend upon you if you would tarry and wait; that this Comforter, the Spirit of Truth, would abide with you forever. Our two rewards for making this choice to receive Him were victorious overcoming and the fact that His joy would remain in us.

Realizing that this experience was not just for Bible characters, I saw that it was custom-made for my immediate need. My heart was stirred and I began to pray. Suddenly I saw with spiritual clarity that while Jesus was here on earth, He was one Person, available only in one location at a time, but when He returned to the unseen world, He sent the Holy Spirit who could be everywhere at the same time.

"You shall receive power when the Holy Spirit has come upon you," said Jesus to His disciples. I read on. After they had received that power, Peter said to the crowds, "For the promise is to you and to your children, and to all who are afar off, as many as the Lord our God will call" (Acts 1:8; 2:39).

At this point in my youth, I was reading a lot of school material to keep up my grade-point average, and I had read the Bible through to get a prize from my dad. But now I began to read, really read the Word for myself. I remembered Peter as the "wimp" who had denied that he was even a friend of Jesus', during the unjust trial when Jesus needed friends the most. What a difference the new dimension of the Holy Spirit made in Peter! It was as though he had received a personality transplant. Shortly after Peter's infusion of the Holy Spirit's power, he had the boldness to preach and three thousand people were converted.

The first Sunday night after school was out that summer, I went to an old-fashioned church in West Terre Haute, Indiana, with my grandparents. After almost everyone had left, I knelt quietly at a seat in the front row to the left of the sanctuary. Some women were sitting nearby, softly singing worship songs. A few men were still kneeling at the altar praying for unsaved loved ones. I began telling Jesus how much I needed the *Parakletos* (the Greek word for "one called alongside to help").

I started to cry, but it was with joy. I began to praise Jesus who sends the gift and thank Him in advance. Then I began to worship in a language that expressed what my limited vocabulary could not. It was joy unspeakable and full of glory! Out of my heart flowed rivers of living water (John 7:38).

I felt a transforming strength fill me like putting a live hand into a limp glove. My life shifted into "overdrive," turbo jet infusion and fuel injection! I have been drawing on that invisible power ever since. It always comes through for me when *my* strength gives up.

The pattern seems to me to go like this: God supplies Jesus, then Jesus sends the Holy Spirit with our supply. He promised that greater works than He did, we shall do, because He goes to His Father who is the Source and sends unending supply in our behalf. When I am writing or working on some other project and my resources run low, I ask for the Holy Spirit's invisible assistance. His help is available upon request.

In John 20:22, we read that Jesus breathed on the disciples and said, "Receive the Holy Spirit." Power. Now, if I had the spirit of Mendelssohn, I could compose music as he did. Had I the spirit of

Shakespeare, I could write poetry as he did. Had I the spirit of Carl Lewis, I could run and jump as I saw him do in the '84 Olympics in Los Angeles. *We have the Spirit of Christ,* and He promised that we could do greater things than He did, because He was going to the Father and sending us "the Promise"!

In this power we can run the race with endurance, and when life meets death, life is resurrection. Jesus promised to do more than we can ask or think according to this power that works in us. Some people live in perpetual crisis, troubled in their minds, never enjoying life. The Holy Spirit is their solution. They can be renewed in the spirit of their minds (that is, renovate their minds) with the mind of Christ, controlled by the Holy Spirit. (See Romans 12:1 and Ephesians 4:23–24.)

At Pentecost in the Upper Room, the Holy Spirit came as "a rushing mighty wind" (Acts 2:2). The night that I received, I felt a gentle breeze blowing undeniably around me, and my spirit soared, lifting me into heavenly places.

I have found many passages where the Spirit is likened to a supernatural wind. Both in the books of Acts and Ezekiel reference is made to the powerful Helper as the wind. "I will cause breath to enter you, and you shall live" (Ezekiel 37:5). "And suddenly there came a sound from heaven, as of a rushing mighty wind, and it filled the whole house" (Acts 2:2).

The Scripture tells us that we can mount up with wings as eagles, run and not be weary, walk and not faint. He will renew our youth as the eagle's.

Episcopal pastor Everett Fullam read these words from Proverbs 30:19, "The way of an eagle in the air," and became engrossed with eagles and the wind. In his book *Where Eagles Soar* he shares its spiritual application. Here is a summary of some of his thoughts.

The eagle usually builds her nest on the face of the cliff where she can utilize the wind and teach her baby eaglets how to use it. When she feels they are ready to soar, she nudges them over the nest's edge each in turn. They try to fly as they fall downward. She is always just below. She swoops down and catches them on

her back, bears them up, puts them back into the nest and repeats
the process again and again. The Holy Spirit, like the mother eagle, is *our* Teacher, *our* Helper. "As an eagle stirs up its nest,
hovers over its young, spreading out its wings, taking them up,
carrying them on its wings," so the invisible Helper teaches us
(Deuteronomy 32:11–12).

It is a phenomenal thought, but an eagle does not really fly. Instead, with an instinctive way of discerning air currents, it locks its
wings and waits for the breeze, for the right breeze. When the right
breeze comes along, the eagle simply *lets go and rides the wind.*

Much is said about the Holy Spirit in the New Testament. The
Old Testament Hebrew word for "wind," *ruach*, is the very same
word as the word for "spirit." The equivalent Greek word *pneuma*
is translated both "wind" and "spirit."

As Terry Fullam explains, eagle Christians are prepared to fly
when they catch the wind of God's Spirit and are borne aloft.
God's work cannot be accomplished, or learned, by human might
and ingenuity. The victorious life is being borne aloft by the
power of God's Spirit. "Those who wait on the Lord shall renew
their strength; they shall mount up with wings like eagles, they
shall run and not be weary, they shall walk and not faint" (Isaiah
40:31). Lord, teach us to wait!

Eagles who soar on the wind are born on the rock, borne up by the
rock, and return to the rock to die. They seem to possess an innate
sense of their own approaching death. When an eagle has a premo-
nition of death, it leaves the nest and flies to the rock. It fastens its
talons to the edge of the rock and looks straight into the setting sun.
When the sun goes down, it dies.

When I was a young mother eagle, making my own nest, one of
my heroes lay dying: my grandfather. He was a carpenter and had
helped build two new houses for my husband and me. I got a call
from Mom Perky, my grandmother. "Dad Perky has been strong
until now, but he seems to be shutting down his equipment. The
doctor was here and says your grandpa won't be here long."

My mother took care of the children, and Dad and I drove down memory lane, through Terre Haute, Indiana, on past West Terre Haute over Sugar Creek, through the burg of Toad Hop, up Larimer Hill and onto a country road. In the edge of the wood is a modest five-room house where my grandparents had lived, loved, gardened; and now it was the rock on the hill where this eagle, my granddad, had fastened his talons to face the setting sun.

When we arrived there he looked good, still brown from working outdoors in his late eighties, a full head of thick, white hair. He reached out one hand from his sickbed and took mine. With the other he gripped my dad's hand. I thought, *He must be scared, frightened of death.* I was wrong. He took our hands to pass on to us a legacy, a heritage. He was born an eagle on the rock. In his later years, he waited for the wind, received the Holy Spirit, and now he was dying like a true eagle. With his eyes open, he raised our hands in his, prayed, then softly and worshipfully whispered, "Jesus," breathed in one deep gasp, then soared on the wind to the eternal Kingdom, his new home.

Christians will never be satisfied until they are soaring. "And you He made alive, who were dead in trespasses and sins, in which you once walked according to the course of this world . . . and were by nature children of wrath. . . . But God, who is rich in mercy, . . . made us alive together with Christ (by grace you have been saved), and raised us up together, and made us sit together in the heavenly places in Christ Jesus" (Ephesians 2:1–6). Before we were born again as eagles, we lived naturally in disobedience. Suddenly the Holy Spirit made the change. He said, "Abide in me, and I in you. Take up residence with Me and God's heart will flow to your hearts, and you will walk and soar as you obey My prompting." He is something like the postman. We may not always see him come, but he leaves evidence behind that he has been here.

I have heard the Holy Spirit referred to as the unction from the Holy One—meaning one who anoints. I have seen this anointing energy come and make a good preacher out of an average one or a good singer out of a poor one. No wonder the Scriptures admonish us to "be strong in the Lord and in the power of His might" (Ephesians 6:10) and to remember that it is " 'not by might nor by power, but by My Spirit,' says the Lord" (Zechariah 4:6).

I have also seen people try to fake the Holy Spirit. It is the difference between the wind and a whirlwind. The wind moves with force and power and produces something. The whirlwind whips around in circles and produces hurricanes and tornados.

The initial experience of the Holy Spirit's coming is a thrill, but is not the end. Ephesians 5:18 says to be filled with, drink deeply of, God's Spirit. He must continue to indwell us and become our teacher as we cooperate with His will. We must ever be learning. Be aware that God has His will for you; the devil has his will for you; and you may also have a will or plan of your own. Sometimes I am my own enemy. When you are not sure about the Holy Spirit's leading, when in doubt about any influence, impulse, intuition, idea or instinct (note that all these words start with *I*), choose the will of God, which never violates the written Word. Immediately the Holy Spirit will come alongside to help you in that choice. There are usually three voices you will hear in every case—God's, Satan's and your own. Say yes to the first (God's) and no to the other two and God will be faithful. He will bring you through—not somehow, but triumphantly!

To be submissive to God's will, to wait for the wind, does not mean to be passive and shift our brains into neutral. We must wait prayerfully before Him, even silently, but listening actively for His voice or for Him to write His Word on our hearts and minds. A satanist medium will wait in a dark room, his whole being perfectly passive. His faculties are dormant, the will "let go" and body relaxed. This absolute passivity is the fundamental law for the working of evil spirits through human beings. They give themselves up or over to evil spirits.

Every time Paul talks of the Holy Spirit in the epistles he makes reference to activity on the part of the believer, active cooperation. God desires fellow workers with Him, not passive, non-thinking instruments. "I also labor, striving according to His working which works in me mightily" (Colossians 1:29).

Study to show yourself approved, filled with truth. Love His Law, His holy Scripture written under the anointing of the Holy Spirit. John tells us that God is light and God is love. No wonder John uses the words *light* and *love* interchangeably, referring to Jesus. He is the Light in the golden throne room and He is the light of the world. The Holy Spirit points to Jesus as He enlightens our understanding and comprehension, leading us into all truth and righteousness.

Early this morning as the sun began coming through the east window of my bedroom, it shone on my computer. I began to think of the many descriptive, doctrinal terms that describe the person, the personality and the ministries of the third Person of the Trinity, the Holy Spirit, the invisible Helper. What I thought would be a few minutes of devotion ended in several hours of thinking, digging into *Strong's* concordance and *Webster's* dictionary. By the end of the second day I had come up with references all the way from *A* to *Z*. Some of them are listed below.

Consider with me. In the Bell Yellow Pages you let your fingers do the walking. In *God's* Yellow Pages, you let the invisible Power do the working!

The Holy Spirit's Yellow Pages

Access: "Through [Jesus] we both have access by one Spirit to the Father" (Ephesians 2:18).

Alpha: The starter, the power package. "They were all filled with the Holy Spirit" (Acts 2:4).

Available to all: "I will pour out My Spirit on all flesh" (Joel 2:28).

Backbone, courage department: Yellow streaks removed, as from Peter, before and after. "Woman, I do not know

Him" (Luke 22:57). "Repent, and . . . be baptized" (Acts 2:38).

Baptizer: "For by one Spirit we were all baptized into one body" (1 Corinthians 12:13).

Breath of God: "He breathed on them, and said to them, 'Receive the Holy Spirit' " (John 20:22).

Co-Creator: "Let Us make man in Our image" (Genesis 1:26).

Comforter: "Walking in the . . . comfort of the Holy Spirit, they were multiplied" (Acts 9:31).

Convicter: "He will convict the world . . ." (John 16:8).

Counselor: "He will guide you into all truth" (John 16:13).

Defense attorney: "It is not you who speak, but the Holy Spirit" (Mark 13:11).

Dove: "[Jesus] saw the Spirit of God descending like a dove" (Matthew 3:16).

Dream-giver: "Your old men shall dream dreams" (Joel 2:28).

Eternal: "The Spirit of God was hovering over the face of the waters" (Genesis 1:2).

Ever-present: "Where can I go from Your Spirit?" (Psalm 139:7).

Financial adviser: "Why . . . lie to the Holy Spirit and keep back part of the price?" (Acts 5:3).

Fire by night: "The Lord went before them . . . by night in a pillar of fire" (Exodus 13:21).

Gentleman: "Let all things be done decently and in order" (1 Corinthians 14:40).

Gift: "How much more will your heavenly Father give the Holy Spirit?" (Luke 11:13).

Guide: "You will guide me with Your counsel" (Psalm 73:24).

Helper: "I will send [the Helper] to you" (John 16:7).

Inspiration: "All Scripture is given by inspiration of God" (2 Timothy 3:16).

Intercessor: "He makes intercession for the saints" (Romans 8:27).

Joy: "[They] were filled with joy and with the Holy Spirit" (Acts 13:52).

Kindness: "The fruit of the Spirit is . . . kindness" (Galatians 5:22).

Leader: "Your ears shall hear a word behind you, saying, 'This is the way' " (Isaiah 30:21).

Means: "Not by might nor by power, but by My Spirit" (Zechariah 4:6).

New wine: "Do not be drunk with wine . . . but be filled with the Spirit" (Ephesians 5:18).

Oil: "The wise took oil . . . with their lamps" (Matthew 25:4).

Paraklete: Greek for *comforter* or *helper.* "He will give you another Helper" (John 14:16).

Personality of God: "They rebelled and grieved His Holy Spirit" (Isaiah 63:10).

Pointer to Jesus: "No one can say that Jesus is Lord except by the Holy Spirit" (1 Corinthians 12:3).

Preacher: "The Spirit of the Lord God is upon Me . . . to preach good tidings to the poor" (Isaiah 61:1).

Promise: "The promise is to you and to your children" (Acts 2:39).

Quickener: "It is the Spirit who gives life" (John 6:63).

Reminder: "He will . . . bring to your remembrance all things that I said to you" (John 14:26).

Revealer: "The Spirit searches . . . the deep things of God" (1 Corinthians 2:10).

Sanctifier: "God . . . chose you for salvation through sanctification by the Spirit and belief in the truth" (2 Thessalonians 2:13).

Songwriter: "Thus says . . . the sweet psalmist of Israel: 'The Spirit of the Lord spoke by me' " (2 Samuel 23:1-2).

Speaker: "I have put My words in your mouth" (Jeremiah 1:9).

Teacher: "The Holy Spirit teaches, comparing spiritual things with spiritual" (1 Corinthians 2:13).

Truth: "The Spirit is truth" (1 John 5:6).

Unction: Unction means spiritual fervor, earnestness, rite of consecration. "You have an anointing from the Holy One" (1 John 2:20).

Unity: ". . . Endeavoring to keep the unity of the Spirit in the bond of peace" (Ephesians 4:3).

Voice: ". . . And after the fire a still small voice" (1 Kings 19:12).

Wind: "There came a sound from heaven, as of a rushing mighty wind" (Acts 2:2).

EXecutive producer of God's eternal power: "[I pray that you would] be strengthened with might through His Spirit in the inner man" (Ephesians 3:16).

Yoke-breaker: "The yoke will be destroyed because of the anointing oil" (Isaiah 10:27).

Zealous: "The zeal of the Lord of hosts shall do this" (2 Kings 19:31).

8

THE UNSEEN WORLD OF MUSIC

We can penetrate the invisible world with our music. I have read that scientists speculate that three percent of light waves, lighting our days, growing our crops, are music waves!

Music we play here is earth's dress rehearsal for the unseen world to come. There will be lots of music and singing in heaven. Can you imagine all the Christian musicians and singers that you have known in your whole lifetime joining with David, the harpist, and all the "greats" from ages past, worshiping around the throne and gathering at the acoustic-perfect Temple in heaven for a grand concert?

Revelation 5:8–13 describes one such scene witnessed prophetically by John. The twenty-four elders each had a harp and they sang a new song. (There will be composing there.)

> I looked, and I heard the voice of many angels around the throne, the living creatures, and the elders; and the number of them was ten thousand times ten thousand, and thousands of thousands, saying with a loud voice: "Worthy is the

Lamb who was slain to receive power and riches and wisdom, and strength and honor and glory and blessing!''
Revelation 5:11–12

I look forward with a great yearning to the time when I will join that throng, not to observe, but to participate.

Perhaps you never had money or time to develop your musical talent. Think of having forever, eternity, to learn from the masters. There will be no inhibition, no one to hold you back, no handicaps there. You will become there what you longed to be here, or will do there what you did here, only in a perfect environment with no hindrance. Disharmony will be an impossibility.

When I lay in a coma in the Terre Haute Union Hospital for 44 days just before I had my experience of seeing the gates of heaven, lingering between life and death, Mary Barton, R.N., placed a *No Visitor* sign on my door and did not allow any noise in my room. Yet during that time I heard celestial strains of music around me, in the room and overhead. I heard voices singing, harmonious, melodious voices of a heavenly choir, and their six-part harmony vibrated and echoed through my body. It cheered my fearful, failing heart and soothed my fractured mind that was so troubled from drugs and pain, so confused from hallucinations and torturous agony. Oh, the glory and power and excitement of that heavenly music! Several times during the coma in my unconscious state, I apparently thanked the nurses for playing that awesome music for me. They told my family, "She keeps hearing music, though we have allowed no noise in her room."

Then, when my body could hold out no longer, at the moment of death, I walked up a hill toward the gate of the capital city of the unseen world now visible to me . . . heaven! I joined the singing voices that were coming over the city's wall. I sang with that celestial choir as I approached the gates. I was able there, finally, to express the feel of music, the beauty, power and range that I had always longed to have on earth. I sang in high, sweet tones, the way I have always yearned to sing. What joyous satisfaction and fulfillment!

Then I stopped singing and listened. I heard Jack Holcomb singing. I recognized his voice. He sang two songs, "I Have Been Born Again" and "The Old Account Was Settled Long Ago." I had heard him sing in concert in Dallas, Texas, and had his record albums.

After my recovery, I called Waco, Texas, to ask Jack to explain this mystery to me. His widow answered the phone and told me that Jack had died some months before. I told her, "I heard your husband sing *there!*" She was delighted, knowing that this was what he would want to do forever. People were doing there what they did here, only in a perfect environment, or becoming there what they were never able to become here on earth.

I know now for sure that music is a powerful connecting rod to the unseen world.

Music is invisible, yet consider its wonderful impact. It has power to stimulate, elevate and inspire. Satan tries to prostitute the purpose of music. He has inspired hell's own music with "backward masking" and hard rock. This is his evil scheme to distract youth, to corrupt their teachable spirits, to sidetrack them and lure them to *his* part of the invisible world—hell's damnation. Music must be a powerful tool for him to work so hard to pervert it.

King David sent singers and musicians ahead before his army, to clear the atmosphere before the fighting began and to cheer the warriors.

After Nehemiah had rebuilt the wall of Jerusalem, he commanded that a certain portion of the city be reserved for the singers, and they were scheduled for singing every day. Their music was also used for the purification of the Temple offerings. (See Nehemiah 11:23; 12:45.)

After the foundation was laid for the Temple, under the leadership of Zerubbabel, construction stopped and the foundation was dedicated with music and singing (Ezra 3:10–11).

And there is no lack of modern-day examples. J.C. Penney lay dying in a hospital bed. In the hallway he heard a Salvation Army lassie singing, "Be not dismayed whate'er betide, God will take care of you." As the invisible influence of music touched his heart, his faith reached up, touched the invisible world and the heart of

God. Jesus healed him and later raised him up to become the prosperous Christian merchant that the world knows.

Modern florists sometimes play soft music in their greenhouses. They feel that it is an unseen stimulus to the growth and blooming of plants.

I read about a survey of reform schools and prisons conducted by a children's psychiatrist. He found that few of the occupants had had any opportunity to study music, sing or play a musical instrument.

As an interesting addendum, he suggested that music can soothe colicky babies. A young mother whose baby suffered colic for six months came to him after she was worn out from patting, petting, kissing, medicating, walking the floor and crying with the baby, from four to nine P.M. each evening religiously. He suggested that she wrap the baby tightly in a warm, soft blanket, tuck her in her crib and play soft music on the record player. It helped soothe her—and her mother—until the colic season was over.

Our friend Inez Bobb directed a "Ladies' Day Apart"—a gathering of teaching and prayer—in Sheridan, Montana. Women had driven great distances to attend the sessions. Midway through the activities of that action-packed day, Inez developed a terrible migraine headache. She said her eyes would not focus and depression set in. She took her medication and went home to rest, but got no relief. "I had to do something, anything," she told me, "so I tried an experiment new to me. I got up and began walking slowly around my living room, first humming, then praising God audibly. Then I prayed asking Jesus to heal me. I sacrificed praise through singing. Soon the headache was gone, and my seminar day successful." A combination of prayer and singing got a quick response.

Ginny Culbertson had been totally healed of MS eight years ago. One morning upon rising, however, she felt the old symptoms trying to come back. She put a cassette tape of worship choruses sung by Paul Hamelink, our church music director, in her player. She saturated her spirit with that uplifting singing the entire day. She is feeling grand again and neither the depression nor the symptoms have returned. "Shallow ditties" don't work, but the kind of music that lifts our spirits to the realm of worship does. This kind of music is therapeutic. Worship is attitude. Worship is the vehicle that gets our prayers airborne!

A resident psychiatrist at the Jamestown Hospital in North Dakota told me, "A patient is not yet hopeless who can be induced to sing or laugh aloud."

Try singing as an antidote to grief. I was touched by the story of a young songwriter and her husband who were eating a picnic lunch beside a tranquil lake in their native Canada. Looking out over the smooth water's surface, they saw a frightening sight. A young boy had fallen out of his overturned boat and was drowning.

The young man kicked off his shoes and dove in to attempt to save the lad. The boy's panic caused them both to drown. The songwriter watched her husband die. For days she thought that she too would die from grief. Early one morning she grabbed the Bible and began searching for comfort. She read that when David's son died, he worshiped God. When Job became acquainted with grief, he worshiped. The young woman, Louisa Stead, took a pen and began writing, worshiping with her gift of songwriting: " 'Tis so sweet to trust in Jesus, just to take Him at His Word. . . . Precious Jesus; oh, for grace to trust Him more!"

What a triumphant song that was and still is! Good things are expensive.

Try singing while you are doing unpleasant chores like sweeping, ironing and washing dishes. Sing away your tension and anxiety. When you sing, you get rid of energy, take your mind off trouble, spark pleasant memories and ease physical tension. Sing in the shower while getting ready to face a hard day. Sing in the car when traffic is bumper-to-bumper at four P.M. and the Honeywell plant has just dismissed its workers. (Why do they call it "rush hour"? It's the time of day when traffic is at a standstill!)

Robert Fulghum's book *All I Really Need to Know, I Learned in Kindergarten* contains a tremendous music story. He explains that when he faces depression and "lows it takes extension ladders to get out of," he turn to his ace in the hole: Beethoven. "I put his Ninth

Symphony on the stereo, pull the earphones down tight, and lie down on the floor. The music comes on like The First Day of Creation.'' Fulghum says he ponders all of Beethoven's troubles—such as his deafness—and with that music booming, ''uplifted, exalted, excited, affirmed, and overwhelmed am I! MANALIVE! Out of [Beethoven's] sorrow and trouble, out of all that frustration and disappointment, out of all that deep and permanent silence, came all that majesty . . . that outpouring of joy and exaltation! He defied his fate with jubilation! And I never can resist all that truth and beauty.''

Singing is good for the heart. You can live longer with a song in your heart while you exercise your body. A physical therapist put twenty professional singers who ranged from ages 28 to 65 through eight minutes of rigorous breathing exercises. Everyone breezed through it. Then he tested a group of forty nonsingers, all of whom were under forty years of age. They struggled to finish the test and their pulse rates skyrocketed.

The invisible power of music has a triple effect. It is therapy for the one singing or playing the music; the person listening receives great positive vibrations; and if your music is worshiping God, it satisfies the heart of your heavenly Father, and causes Him in return to interpret your heart song and grant your petition.

When I was about eleven years old, my parents gave me an accordion for Christmas. We lived in the country, and many times out of pure boredom I would sway back and forth in the porch swing, practicing my accordion lessons. As my little brothers grew, I would strap that accordion onto my chest and flee to the orchard for privacy. There I could express my feelings and worship God by playing that accordion out in the open air under the trees. Music became my insurance policy against frustration; it also helped me resist the temptation to walk the streets or experiment with smoking or drugs. After a little music appreciation class ''out there,'' I would return to the house merrily, willing to help with dishes, set the table or care for the younger children.

My father was chaplain for the jail and nursing homes. He would take me and my "portable piano" with him. I didn't particularly want to go, but the music brought smiles to the depressed prisoners and the ill old people, and after I had put approximately 12,000 miles on that musical instrument, the message got through to me. I was not only helping others, I was helping myself through the vehicle of joy—music.

Now, not just any song will do. Pick songs like "Amazing Grace," "Joy Unspeakable," "In Moments Like These," "When Answers Aren't Enough," "Jesus Is Coming Again" or "Sunlight in My Soul."

Every creature is born with the need to worship. Birds and human beings alike worship the Creator by whistling or singing. I have sat in Ruth Eckerd Hall here in Clearwater and felt my soul soar and my scalp tingle while listening to the wonderful sounds and feeling the stirring vibrations of the London Symphony Orchestra. I have gotten that same thrill and been elevated from a melancholy mood by listening to the birds outside my writing studio window. Have you noticed that first thing in the morning birds tune up to God by whistling their tunes? And the last thing before they tuck their little heads under their feathery wings to slumber, they sing Him their last contribution of worship. How much merrier would our human hearts be if we would learn from the songbirds!

I have a cassette tape called "Celestial Reflections" by Marge Carlson. This petite, affectionate blonde and her husband live in Fullerton, California. She loves expressing her feelings and worshiping God while whistling softly. A sound expert helped the Carlsons discover that many songbirds, such as the mockingbird, sing fourteen distinct songs, and they all sing in the key of E flat. With the help of orchestral accompaniment, Marge performs whistling solos in concert, all in the key of E flat.

All nature is orchestrated to express musical praise to the Creator. Even my cat. His throat trembles pleasantly, his musical expression of contentment and appreciation for life, much like the idling of a well-tuned car.

God desires our worship and our praise and one of the most

meaningful ways to express it is through music. It is a universal imperative (Exodus 20:3–6; Matthew 4:10; Luke 19:37–40; John 4:23). We are rehearsing for the invisible world. Heaven is now and will be evermore filled with the sounds of worship and praise—with voices sounding like trumpets (Revelation 4:1) and harps plinking (Revelation 5:8) and such sustained singing (Revelation 5:9) that times of silence are apparently unusual enough to be noted (Revelation 8:1). Ezekiel, Isaiah and John in Revelation confirm these facts.

Worship is more than an activity; it is an attitude. It is to experience reality, to touch life and the supernatural. It is to know, to feel, to experience Jesus. As Richard Foster has explained, worship is breaking into the shekinah of God, even being invaded by the shekinah of God. Shekinah is the glory or radiance of God dwelling in the midst of His people. It denotes the immediate presence of God.

William Temple puts it this way: To worship is to quicken the conscience by the holiness of God, to feed the mind with the truth of God, to purge the imagination by the beauty of God, to open the heart to the love of God, to devote the will to the purpose of God.

"Enter into His gates with thanksgiving, and into His courts with praise" (Psalm 100:4). We quote this Scripture frequently. Just as a grocery store has an automatic sliding door to let you and your cart enter, thanksgiving opens the gate. Then singing praise opens the court where you go into the throne room to make your request known. Praise and worship are the finest, purest forms of petition.

How natural music is! It evolves from the soul and the mind. Even young children express themselves freely and naturally through music and rhythm. We should become like children: They find it so easy to hum, tap, clap, dance, sing with joy, express frivolity!

Music is probably the most basic and classic form of expression. It is the drama of the heart. Beethoven was deaf, but heard music from his "inner ear" and wrote it down. Historians have stated that Martin Luther won more converts to Christ through his encouragement of congregational singing than through his strong preaching and teaching. Of the Wesleys it was said that for every person they won with their preaching, ten were won through their music. A spiritual church is a singing church.

Language uses words to try to explain how we feel, but language, no matter how hard we try, cannot express the complete feeling of life. That is the role of music. Music does for our feelings what language does for our thoughts.

Spoken or written words enter the ear or eye gate and are processed through the brain. But music skips the "thinking" process and goes directly to the heart, transcending the intellect and touching the soul. God reaches us this way. And, in turn, music will allow *you* to express to God that which cannot be put into words. Without it, your relationship with Him will be reduced to an intellectual exchange.

If God walked here on earth, we could hug Him and show Him love and honor as we do our earthly fathers. It is truly wonderful that He has provided a means of expression in music.

In 1 Samuel 16 we read the story of King Saul who was troubled in spirit. His counselors brought David, the shepherd/musician, before him, and as he played the harp Saul would become settled. In this case music was doing what it was created to do, minister to the unseen part of a man, his soul and spirit. The power of music touches a world that is outside of what is seen or understood with logic. No amount of logic could relieve Saul of his troubled spirit, because his was not an intellectual need. Music was the key to touching Saul's feelings, which was where his problem lay. The music David played embodied feelings that were quite different from those Saul was experiencing. His soul was eased and music's purpose was accomplished.

Music clarifies and expresses when words cannot. You will always find music in places where emotions are high. Perhaps the most emotion-filled moment in Scripture is when the virgin Mary becomes aware that she is carrying the child Messiah! She bursts forth into a song that we now know as the Magnificat, or Song of

Mary (Luke 1:46–55). Hannah responded the same way as she made the sacrifice of leaving her miracle son at the Temple (1 Samuel 2:1–10). Miriam sang when God delivered the children of Israel at the Red Sea and drowned Pharaoh's army (Exodus 15). We may make a conscious decision to serve God, but God created us for a much more profound relationship than intellect alone can allow. Frankly, our intellect is no match for God's anyway. As we worship God in song, our emotions touch and we develop strong emotional ties with the Almighty!

We, like David, can do for ourselves or others what he did for Saul. Read aloud or sing the Psalms; you will touch God, and He through heaven's tuning fork, music, will touch and bring joy down to your soul, too.

Those who are not able to express feeling are not emotionally healthy. If our emotions are troubled, we will surely have problems in other areas of our being. Music is necessary, therefore, for spiritual, intellectual and physical health.

With fond memories I look back into my earliest teen years and remember such an emotional expression of words in the old hymn "The Love of God."

Could we with ink the ocean fill,
And were the skies of parchment made,
Were every stock on earth a quill, and every man a scribe by trade,
To write the love of God above would drain the ocean dry.
Nor could the scroll contain the whole, though stretched from sky to sky!
Oh love of God, how rich and pure, how measureless and strong!
It shall forevermore endure, the saints' and angels' song.

After we have bargained with God, reasoned, contemplated, pulled rank, even "threatened" Him with His own Scripture, there are times when we have exhausted every other approach and yet can still sing with the understanding and the Spirit.

When our logical minds cannot pray to God appropriately, our musical praise wafts heavenward! Praise is the vehicle that gets our petition airborne.

My earthly father, Glenn Perkins, learned this and passed on a powerful legacy of "how to" touch God. It happened during one of the fiercest of storms in the life of our family.

Before I was born, my mother and dad went to see the movie "Sonny Boy." They just knew they were expecting a baby boy and decided to give him a proper name, but call him "Sonny Boy." When I arrived instead, a skinny, wrinkled preemie daughter, they named me Betty.

A few years later my baby brother came along. It was the end of the Depression, and we were living in a humble three-room house on Lee Avenue in West Terre Haute, Indiana. It belonged to my great-grandmother Burns. We were poor, and though electricity was available, we could not afford it. Phones were in vogue, but we could not pay to have one installed.

One wintry night during a snowstorm the baby boy, Don, became desperately ill with meningitis. He had an extremely high fever and went into convulsions. My dad bundled up and struggled through the blinding, blowing snow to the nearest home that had a telephone only to learn that our doctor, the one M. D. who would see a patient without funds, was not home.

My dad returned weary and discouraged. No one we knew owned a car. There seemed to be no way to find help.

I lay in my bed, but couldn't sleep for little Don's pitiful wailing. He even refused to nurse Mother's breast. Mother walked him for hours, trying to comfort him. They tried to bathe his fever down, but to no avail. I remember how frightened they were. At one point I put my pillow over my head so I could not hear the baby's pitiful cries.

Daddy insisted that Mother lie down and get some rest. He told her, "I'll take over for a while, till morning and daylight. Then we'll be able to see and go for help. Try to get some sleep."

My dad cried and begged God to help baby Don. I listened while he quoted Scriptures and made some promises to the Lord. Looking through the doorway into the living room, I could see into the darkened room by the streetlight just outside the window. My dad bundled the baby tightly in a little flannel blanket, then started pacing the floor slowly, holding the little face under his chin and neck, and he hummed and talked to him. Suddenly the baby stiffened, then went limp across my dad's arm. Even in the dim light I could see the panic on Daddy's face. Then cuddling him near his chest my dad started saying, "Bless the name of Jesus. Praise You, Lord. I worship You. In everything I give You thanks." What a strange thing to do in such a dire emergency! I wondered briefly if he were crazed with fear and worry.

Then he did something I rarely heard him do. He started singing pitifully. Now Dad always sang pitifully. The music we children have been gifted with came from the Burns side of the family, not his Perkins side. Dad took banjo lessons once, and we all begged him to quit. He had no talent for rhythm, timing or harmony . . . but tonight he sang for all he was worth:

> Reach out and touch the Lord as He goes by.
> You'll find He's not too busy to hear your heart's cry.
> He's passing by this moment, your need He'll supply.
> Reach out and touch the Lord as He goes by.

Mother came out of the bedroom in her pink rosebud flannel granny gown, crying from prayer, to see a horrid sight. As she lit a lamp they gasped and looked at each other with blank, helpless expressions. The baby had turned blue.

Dad cradled him again in the curve of his arm and began walking slowly, and I shall *never forget* the power of music and the vehicle of praise that got his petition airborne! Dad starting singing again— not timidly, but with great confidence.

> The Great Physician now is near—the sympathizing Jesus.
> He stoops the fainting heart to cheer; oh, hear the voice of Jesus.
> Sweetest note in seraph song, sweetest name on mortal tongue,
> Sweetest carol ever sung, Jesus, blessed Jesus!

My dad continued to worship loudly. I held my breath as the moments passed. Then, miraculously, baby Don opened his eyes. He smiled, he cooed sweetly and drank a little milk. The fever broke, his color returned and he fell into a sound sleep and awakened just after dawn, my playful, happy baby brother.

When we were finally able to contact Aunt Lillian (a schoolteacher with a car) and visit Doctor Shanklin, he remarked, "It's the most unexplainable, dramatic recovery from meningitis I've ever witnessed."

Oh, the impact of music and rejoicing! "He sent his word, and healed them. . . . Oh that men would praise the Lord for his goodness, and for his wonderful works to the children of men! And let them sacrifice the sacrifices of thanksgiving, and declare his works with rejoicing" (Psalm 107:20–22, KJV).

From time to time we get samples from the unseen world sent down to earth. We don't get streets of gold here, or a tree with twelve fruits, but we do get music.

For years I exchanged journalism ideas with an old friend, Helen Leckrone, a columnist in Salem, Illinois. She had a knack for making her own greeting cards with her personal logo in fine print: "ho–made–by–helen."

Three days after her death, I received a note from one of Helen's neighbors. They found one of her original Christmas cards—ho–made—stamped and addressed to me, lying on her desk.

The message printed by hand was:

I wish you a Happy, Holy Christmas and pray God will shower you with His richest blessings in the New Year! Conditions in the world grow more ungodly, but I sing a song my mother used to sing, "We Have an Anchor," and I stay calm and happy. (Oh, the power of God's music!)

Love, Helen Leckrone

Folded inside the card was a photocopy of the old song "We Have an Anchor" and in parentheses she had scrawled boldly with a red magic marker: *"We do have an Anchor."* Thank You, Jesus.

When our eyes behold thro' the gathering night
The city of gold, our harbor bright,
We shall anchor fast by the heav'nly shore,
With the storms all past forevermore.
We have an anchor that keeps the soul
Steadfast and sure while the billows roll,
Fastened to the Rock which cannot move,
Grounded firm and deep in the Savior's love.

Jesus is the recurring theme in the symphony of the unseen world! While closing this chapter, I found myself first humming, then breaking out in audible singing, the little chorus the Scottish family Cameron taught me: "Never a reason strong enough for not praising the Lord." It ends with this good counsel:

Praise Him, you can never afford
To ever stop praising the Lord!

Note: Much of the valuable input of this chapter was given to me by a young woman who teaches music in North Carolina, who asked to remain anonymous, and our music director at church, Paul Hamelink. Mr. Hamelink is presently working on his doctorate at the University of South Florida in Tampa.

9
LINKS TO THE INVISIBLE KINGDOM

I am excited by the way God in His unseen, overruling, practical providence, leads us from this world to the invisible Kingdom by building us bridges and links, many of which span the gaps of life.

"Be not conformed to this world: but be ye transformed by the renewing of your mind, that ye may prove what is that good, and acceptable, and perfect will of God" (Romans 12:2).

In chapter 4 I described the main link we as God's creatures have with the Father—prayer. There are others that I would like to discuss here briefly including dreams, visions, Scripture, God's voice, an inner witness, circumstances, exhorters, balcony people, door openers and even hornets.

Dreams and Visions

My daydream of being a writer started at the age of eight. That dream became a reality at 41 when my first book *My Glimpse of Eternity* was published. To date, it has sold two million copies in various editions and in eighteen languages. The road was a long one starting west of Sugar Creek, by the burg of Toad Hop near Terre Haute, Indiana, and ending in Clearwater, Florida.

I am not the only humble human being who dreamed that dream long before it became a reality. Sometimes on the journey from here to the unseen world, our dreams can sustain us. So it was with the renowned missionary, William Carey. While he mended shoes, he kept for years a map of the world tacked to the front of his cobbler's bench, in full view. We tend to follow our gaze.

You have a certain number of years on the journey between this temporary world and the invisible Kingdom. While, in view of eternity, the number may not seem so lengthy, still, on a day-to-day basis you may feel the gap between is long and hard. When you need encouragement, think of Joseph. The bridge between Joseph's dream and the reality was a long one, but Joseph made it and you can make it! Keep in mind that the Lord is in complete command of your situation. His timing is different from ours because we want relief right now. His vision for us is eternal and concerns the invisible Kingdom.

Paul Billheimer, author of *Destined for the Throne*, also wrote the story of *Joseph, The Mystery of God's Providence*.

This Israeli lad went from the bottom of a well in Dothan to become prime minister of Egypt. Along the journey he was misunderstood, sold into slavery, imprisoned, released, and for refusing to make love to the wife of one of the king's officers, he was misunderstood and imprisoned again.

While in prison, Joseph received help from the invisible world (wisdom from above), interpreted the king's dreams and was elevated to the number two spot in Egypt. His dream not only sustained him for thirteen years, it brought him to the position where he could sustain life for his starving father and the brothers who had sold him into slavery in the first place. We can learn in the deepest sloughs that God is in full control, and we can say with Joseph, someone may have "meant evil against me; but God meant it for good" (Genesis 50:20)

Every gap will become plain in the glorious light of His revelation. We like Joseph are being groomed for rulership in the invisible Kingdom. Every born-again believer can be a king in training for a throne.

Walk with patience your bridge from earth to eternity and allow God time to develop you for rulership. A mushroom comes up overnight, but it requires a hundred years for a mighty oak tree to mature. No wonder some of the "greats" of the Bible lived 900 years!

Scripture

The Word, Holy Scripture, is also a link to the invisible Kingdom. On life's journey, "we walk by faith and not by sight." His Word is our all-sufficient guide. "I will . . . perform My good word toward you," to give you an expected end—what you believe for (Jeremiah 29:10–11).

George Muller, who through faith and prayer founded a series of remarkable orphanages in England in the nineteenth century, was a dishonest boy and put in jail at age sixteen. Out of boredom he began reading the Bible. The Word convicted him. Seventy years later at 86 he was still preaching. The last song he sang at church was:

> We'll sing of the Shepherd that died,
> That died for the sake of the flock,
> His love to the utmost was tried,
> And immovable stood as a rock.

The following morning after a cup of tea and a biscuit, he died. An old friend described his going to the invisible World: "Dear old Mr. Muller, just slipped quietly off Home as the gentle Master opened the door and whispered, 'Come.' " In his life, the Word made the difference between his life at the beginning and life at the end.

God would not have us come as ignorant children when we petition Him, but as ambassadors to His home government. He would have us come boldly to the throne of grace, connected to Him by the "cable" of well-reasoned scriptural understanding and Kingdom purpose, praying earnestly, but intelligently.

A friend of Hudson Taylor once said of him, "Taylor knows the Word and the Word knows Taylor. The Lord has had His way so long with Hudson Taylor, that now Hudson Taylor can have his way with the Lord." That's being linked to the invisible Kingdom!

God's Voice

Sometimes when one of His earth children is in great need, God bridges the gaps of life by speaking in His own audible voice from the unseen world.

Roxanne Brant wrote a pamphlet, "Knowing God's Will for Your Life," which contained these two stories that touched me.

A young mother was awakened suddenly from a sound sleep by God's voice: *Check the baby.* She arose and went quickly into the nursery in the adjoining room. The baby was blue and gasping, the covers bound around its tiny head, but God awakened the attentive mother just in time to avert tragedy.

A man had stopped his car at a busy traffic intersection. The light turned green, but the voice said, *Keep your foot on the brake; don't go.* Everyone began honking for him to proceed, but he listened to God's voice. Suddenly racing downhill through that crowded intersection at high speed came a truck with brake failure bursting through the red light. But for one driver who heard God's voice and obeyed, the truck could have smashed into cars, killing many.

Circumstances

Many times God uses circumstances to link us to the unseen world. Some months ago I had a call from a young man who pastors a church in the shadow of a large church in southern California. He asked me to come and give my healing/resurrection story, hoping to bring in visitors and increase his attendance.

When I arrived there he asked me to have an anointing service. "This has never been done in our denomination," he told me. "I would probably be put out if I did it myself. I just want you to know this ahead of time. If I get called onto the green carpet for it, I'll tell them that you were a guest speaker, not of our denomination." I almost got back on the plane. I'm no magician. I'm not even a minister.

In my room before the service, I knelt and prayed, "Lord, this is an awkward situation. Cover it by Your mercy and grace. Come to our rescue. Let me do only what You want and no more."

At the close of my presentation that evening, I asked the minister to stand by me. I held up a small bottle of olive oil, explaining the verses in James 5, and invited anyone to come forward who wished to be prayed for.

I waited for what seemed to me a long time. Finally I decided to give the benediction, but when I raised my head and opened my eyes, an ancient man was helping an old lady (his wife) down the aisle toward us with the aid of a walker. When he leaned forward I thought he wanted to be prayed for, so I anointed him. At this point I didn't know he was leaning forward to whisper some instructions about his wife. Just as well anyway. I put a drop of olive oil on his forehead. He literally screamed at me, "Not me, *she* is the one who's sick! I just came to help her." Well, it was too late. What could I do, rub the oil off?

So I anointed his wife, too, and putting a hand on each of them prayed, "O Lord Jesus, meet every need, answer the heart's cry for this woman." The husband interrupted me, screaming again. "My God! I can hear!" He had been healed by accident. Then he asked in a quiet voice, "Does Jesus really heal unbelievers?"

God through circumstances had built a bridge to this man from the unseen world, even though the man had never even tried to reach

God. He came to the meeting only to please his sick wife. God's love can be the link from Him to the unloving.

Other circumstances may seem even stranger, but could well be His hand at work bridging the gap to the invisible kingdom. In Exodus 23:28 we read that the Lord used a swarm of hornets to drive out the Hivite, the Canaanite and the Hittite from the land, opening the way for the Israelites to inherit Canaan. The Israelites did not have to fight with a bow or sword in that instance, God used His little critters—an odd circumstance in a battle. (See also Joshua 24:12)

Inner Witness

My husband quotes a proverb that he originated: "Always do what you can't always do."

A number of years ago he was a missionary-teacher at a theological seminary he founded in Egypt. One morning during prayer (the year was 1967), he had a feeling that would not go away. That inner voice or inward witness prompted him to pack all his family's belongings in barrels, and apply for passport visas back to the United States. He went to the American consulate, who told him, "Fear is a way of life here. Unrest is the norm. We see no immediate danger. Forget it. Stay here."

Carl decided to obey that inner urge, that Holy Spirit nudge. The three passes to him, his wife and daughter were the last given on the Italian *Marconi*, the last ship that left the Suez Canal before it was bombed during the Six-Day War with Israel.

God will build a bridge between Himself and you, in whatever way He chooses—dreams and visions, Scripture, His voice, an inner witness or maybe circumstances—but He will reach you.

Jesus endured the cross because He was linked to eternity. He desires for you to be there as well and will lead us by the touch of His hand.

Will those who come behind us find us faithful? Let's draw a clear map, build a secure bridge for the lambs who follow.

10
THE INVISIBLE ENEMY

When Satan fell from heaven, where did he go? Where is he now? I believe he and his dark angels are headquartered in the second heaven, in between this earth world and the invisible world to come, looking to establish his evil domain. He with his demon followers lingers in that atmosphere trying to hinder your prayers from ascending to the throne of God. He goes to and fro on the earth, walking up and down, stalking, hoping to invade your heart (see Job 1 and 2).

I am much more interested in lifting Jesus than putting down the devil. I refuse to give Satan valuable time when I'm on television, or space in my books. The media has given him far too much free publicity already. This chapter is merely to inform and warn so that we will be aware of his tactics and evil schemes.

My uncle Earl Rodgers did biblical research to better understand the cunning of Satan. He has titled it "The Hiss of Dis." Let's talk about "old dis." *Dis* in *Webster's* dictionary is the Greek mythology counterpart of Pluto. He is the god of the lower part of Hades. *Dis* means the opposite or reverse of. In medical terms we think of disease and dysfunction, things painful, faulty, bad or difficult. The devil is the accuser, the adversary, the opponent, the arch enemy of good, in opposition to God and from Hades.

James speaking of Jesus said, "He gives more grace." Old "dis" brought disgrace. God wants us to have favor with God and man; Satan has brought disfavor and causes dislike.

Paul tells us that we should please God. Satan urged Eve to displease God. Satan causes us to be disagreeable, makes us discouraged. He brings disappointment.

We are admonished to wear robes of righteousness. The father put a robe on the Prodigal Son, a mark of dignity. Satan would disrobe us, strip us bare, reveal our secrets, bring us to shame. He would try to cause us to disobey the commandments, bringing discomfort, implanting his evil disposition.

Jesus bring contentment; Satan brings discontentment, disease, disrespect, disfavor, disrepute. He sews discord bringing disunity to the Body of Christ. Almost any word with the prefix dis can be applied to the character of Satan. He would have us disagree, brings disorder and wants us to disregard our consecration.

The devil is the author of confusion. He takes on many disguises. Our invisible weapon for the unseen enemy is described in 2 Corinthians 10:4: "The weapons of our warfare are not carnal but mighty in God for pulling down [the enemy's] strongholds, casting down arguments and every high thing that exalts itself against the knowledge of God, bringing every thought into captivity to the obedience of Christ."

If you are traveling on the wrong road, God will help you make a U-turn. Christ is the only way to heaven; all other paths are detours of doom. The denial of sin is the devil's chloroform. "Be reconciled to God."

There is a war going on, right now, of unseen forces. Jesus said that the enemy came to destroy, but Jesus came that we might have life (John 10:10). "Be sober, be vigilant; because your adversary the devil, as a roaring lion, walketh about, seeking whom he may devour" (1 Peter 5:8, KJV). Jesus told us, "I have overcome the world. . . . I come quickly! Hold fast what you have [give Satan no ground], that no one may take your crown . . . I am coming quickly, and My reward is with Me'' (John 16:33; Revelation 3:11; 22:12).

The angel Lucifer held a high position in God's Kingdom and had access to all the heavenlies upon the holy mountain of God and also Eden, the Garden of God. He was beautiful, but became corrupted by pride in his wisdom and brightness. "How you are fallen from heaven, O Lucifer, son of the morning! How you are cut down to the ground, you who weakened the nations! For you have said in your heart: 'I will ascend into heaven, I will exalt my throne above the stars of God . . . I will be like the Most High.' Yet you shall be brought down to Sheol, to the lowest depths of the Pit'' (Isaiah 14:12–15).

When Lucifer stopped praising God and began to praise himself, he was dismissed from heaven. I believe there is a caution here for us. Humility is recognizing that God is responsible for the achievements in our lives. "And what do you have that you did not receive? . . . Why do you glory as if you had not received it? (1 Corinthians 4:7).

When Satan was dismissed, he started a war. Immediately God commissioned Michael the archangel as commander-in-chief of the armies of heaven. There was a battle in which Satan and one-third of the angels who fought with him were thrown out of heaven (Revelation 12). God still has the two-thirds majority. The good angels ("innumerable hosts," Hebrews 12:22) outnumbered the evil, dark angels.

Mona Johnian and her husband, Paul, founded a teaching center in Winchester, Massachusetts. She has done extensive study on this subject, and I appreciate her research and agree with her findings about the three heavens. The first heaven is the atmosphere around the earth where airplanes and birds fly. The second heaven is the starry kingdom that contains the galaxies. The third heaven is the highest, containing the throne of God and our eternal home. This is where Lucifer fell from. It is also the place that Paul was "translated" to and described for us.

Satan's evil character is the source of anarchy and rebellion in the universe.

In the beginning Satan beguiled Adam and Eve's simplicity (2 Corinthians 11:3) and he has been trying to complicate the lives of Christians ever since. He is trying to disconnect us from God. He wants to disengage our life-support system from the Source of life eternal.

The first lie that Satan told is the same one he is using today and also the last one he will tell just before Jesus comes again. The serpent told Eve that she would not die if she disobeyed and ate the fruit, but "you will be like God" (Genesis 3:5), tricking her with the very desire that had caused his own downfall! There is a movement today quoting this Scripture word for word. Be warned: The world is not getting perfect. *We are not becoming gods.* There is only one God.

Sometimes Satan pounces on us when we are down, but many times he slips up on our blind side. He will take advantage during depression and he can take greater advantage when we prosper. There is an illusion to success. As we learn from Eden, he will even try to take advantage in a perfect setting.

Consider the atmosphere where he approached Eve. She was not an underprivileged or abused child or torn apart by divorce. She did not feel inferior to other women: She was the only female on earth. She did not know about jealousy or competition or overwork, yet she yielded to restless suggestions of the devil.

But thank God, from among her descendants would come forth a Child, and "of the increase of His government and peace there will be no end" (Isaiah 9:7).

Satan stepped into high gear to try and destroy that Child. Since the day Satan fell with his angels he has rallied forces to try to distract mankind from truth, the path of life and the eternal kingdom. He tried to deceive Adam. I believe there was a huge battle of unseen cosmic forces going on in the second heaven the night of Christ's birth. I believe, first of all, that the devil rallied his evil angels to try to prevent the message from getting to earth.

But the angel of the Lord came upon the shepherds and the glory of the Lord shone 'round about them, and the angel said, "Fear not." (This is bad news for the devil, but good news for mankind.) "Behold, I bring you good tidings of great joy for all people. The Savior is born, the Son of the Living God, Christ the Lord. Suddenly there was a victory shout and there appeared with the angel a multitude of the heavenly host praising God and saying, 'Glory to God in the highest and on earth, peace, good will toward men' " (Luke 2:8–14, paraphrase).

Satan didn't give up. He implanted hate and jealousy in Herod's heart to destroy the baby Jesus, without success. He appeared to Jesus after His baptism and tempted, harassed Him. If the devil has the arrogance, the nerve to tempt Jesus, the perfect Son of God, you can be sure he is going to try to deceive you and me.

"Do not think it strange concerning the fiery trial which is to try you, as though some strange thing happened to you" (1 Peter 4:12). This is par for the course. Satan will hack at the heels of any person who is doing or is about to be commissioned to do some great thing for his God. "Resist him, steadfast in the faith, knowing that the same sufferings are experienced by your brotherhood in the world" (1 Peter 5:9). In other words, this is not uncommon.

Just keep in mind that when Jesus' blood flowed on the cross, Satan lost the war, and he has only two tools left to use on us. They are deception and bluff. "Resist the devil and he will flee from you" (James 4:7). If you know how he is coming against you, you can address it directly:

"Stand back, you foul opposing spirit of deception [for example]. I rebuke you in the name of Jesus, by the authority of the blood of Calvary. I command you to go back to the pit whence you came and be sealed there permanently." The Word promises us that "when the enemy comes in like a flood, the Spirit of the Lord will lift up a standard against him" (Isaiah 59:19).

In an earlier chapter I told of Ann Morrison's miraculous healing. The Monday following she was awakened with a horrible fear. Satan, old "dis," tried to *dis*connect her from peace and health. She feared that her family would think her a fanatic for not needing them, now that she was well, and would turn away from her and reject her. She was wise in calling her prayer partners and her pastor to come and sit in her house praying with her. Her spirit lifted and she is still walking in health and victory.

The least used, most needed power source against the invisible enemy is prevailing prayer. Joshua went down in history as "winning the battle," but it was Moses the intercessor who really "won the war' " (Exodus 17:8–13).

Jesus' blood prevails and drives Satan away. When the seventy returned to Jesus with their triumphant stories of overpowering demons, Jesus said, "I saw Satan fall like lightning from heaven" (Luke 10:17–18). He fell and he falls when we submit to God. Rebuke him by reminding him of Jesus' blood, reminding him of his past fall and reminding him of his future fall when he will be bound and cast into hell forever (Revelation 20:10).

I received a letter from a soldier stationed at Fort Riley, Kansas. In it he says, "Betty, I forgot to keep wearing the armor of Jesus Christ and found that I alone was no match for the devil. He has an IQ of 5,000 and mine is only 139. But I utilized the blood of Jesus Christ, and I have become victorious again!"

I know of a minister and his wife who went overseas to minister. Their children were left at their farm, in the loving care of grandparents. Many people were getting saved, delivered and healed by their work. The first night following that glorius meeting, the devil appeared to the minister in a dream and threatened him.

Sounds kept thundering in his ears: *I am going to kill your children. I have put rabies in the foxes that live in the woods adjoining your property. They will bite your children and they will die.*

He called together some Christians who joined with his wife and him and he prayed this: "Satan, you're a liar. My children belong to Jesus. I resist your threats. Our property has been dedicated to God. I have a covenant with God in the blood of His Son Jesus; therefore, my children, my entire household and my possessions are insured by that bloodline that protects us from danger and harm."

A short while later they received a letter from the grandparents.

It read: "Today we were walking around the farm and found five dead foxes in different locations. They seemed to have attempted to come on your property, but just fell over dead. It was such a curious situation, we called the veterinarian. An autopsy concluded that all five foxes had died with rabies."

Nothing can cross the bloodline of Jesus!

My husband and I are aware of this unseen foe. More than once we have had to "plead the blood" and resist the enemy against the "Saturday night syndrome." It seems that some misunderstanding or interruption will *always* come Saturday evening to disrupt our peace and effectiveness to minister on Sunday. We have become aware of his "accusing" tactics. We quit blaming each other now and blame the enemy of our souls. He was having his "evil fun" pitting us against each other. We bound ourselves together and "have just begun to fight."

Our invisible enemy realized that if he could destroy our tranquility and separate us, Saturdays or otherwise, our joy and creativity would "leak out," leaving us spiritually anemic. Then who would want to listen to Carl's sermons, and who could enjoy reading my books? We've gotta make it with God's help.

We are not ignorant of Satan's devices and tricks (2 Corinthians 2:11). He would like to prevent me from writing a chapter like this one that exposes him as the invisible enemy. He has not used visible roadblocks, but hurdles like solicitors at the door frequently . . . pranksters . . . wrong numbers . . . distractions . . . depression . . . and almost-quarrels. Satan is a robber, and he is subtle. He tried to bring division in heaven, and he tries to bring division on earth, especially in families. Don't let him. Start swinging your fine, sharp, two-edged sword of faith and stand in the power of the blood, coupled with prayer and the Word.

Satan makes his arrows bright, but his way in the end is dark and slippery. There are no exits in hell. The decision must be made in this life to choose God.

The Word instructs us to follow the straight and narrow way. At the airport there are many gates if you want to go anywhere, but if you know your destination, you must enter the right jetway.

I was late for choir practice one evening and got behind a line of slow-moving beach traffic of swimmers, boaters and surfers. Disgusted, I tried for a shortcut to save time and ended up behind a deserted service station, the graveyard for discarded cars. I was reminded that "there is a way which seems right to a man, but its end is the way of death" (Proverbs 14:12).

There is in all of us an instinct of revolt, a rebel who accepts no yoke. This element of independence is the root of all sin. Sin, unseen then, all but flows in the blood of our veins. Temptation is not sin. But as we let ourselves dwell on a small germ of temptation, it grows and too often rules our behavior.

If you have sinned, repent, take hold of yourself and stop doing the transgression. Like a piece of hot iron, drop it! Avoid anything that would separate you from the love of God, that would alienate you from loving people, that would violate the instruction of the Word of God.

The enemy can bring about restlessness in a job, covetousness of a bigger house. We must take inventory, stay plugged into the Source, the authority, our God. We must stay in tune through prayer. Satan sows seeds of discord in the fertile soil of bitterness, sin, stubbornness, pride. Guard against the evil gardener. Let the *Word* dwell in you richly.

No one would think of playing professional football without the pads, helmet, teeth guard, etc. Don't go to war without your unseen armor of God: the helmet of salvation, the breastplate of righteousness, the sword of the Spirit, the shield of faith, girding your loins with truth and your feet with the preparation of the gospel of peace. With your armor, and with the blood of Jesus to cover you, you will be able to withstand in the evil day (Ephesians 6:10–18).

In the book *Born for Battle*, R. Arthur Matthews uses an army illustration: On the Omaha Beachead, June 6, 1944, all the men had been trained in the use of their weapons, yet only one man in four actually made use of his firepower. Having a weapon is not enough.

We must *use* it. Having the skill and hitting the bull's eye on the practice range is not enough. We have the weapons of warfare through prayer to tear down the enemy's stronghold. We must *use* our prayer power.

One of our chief weapons is praise. The only time there was war in heaven was when Satan decided to get praise for himself instead of praising Jesus. When you stop praising God you are vulnerable to Satan's attack. When you praise God two things happen: One, you exalt Jesus high above the earth; and two, if there is a little rebel in you, you will be glad to know that when you praise God, you are reminding the devil of his defeat.

Most Christians are not aware of the struggle between divine and evil forces in this world. They haven't located the battlefield where the war will be won or lost in their personal lives. The battlefield is clear: the mind (2 Corinthians 10:3–6).

Beware "lest Satan should take advantage of us; for we are not ignorant of his devices" (2 Corinthians 2:11). We know his wiles all too well. The word *wiles* means witchlike divination, a trick or stratagem intended to ensnare or deceive, luring or enticing by a magic spell. The Bible warns and makes us aware of his intentions, methods, schemes, designs, purposes, intentions and tricks. The devil is after you. Don't play into his hands. He never quits.

"He departed from Him until an opportune time" (Luke 4:13). Satan only left Jesus alone for a while. When Jesus was arrested in Gethsemane He said, "This is your hour, and the power of darkness (Luke 22:53).

Our victory today depends on Christ's death and resurrection. This was the purpose of the incarnation. "The Son of God was manifested, that He might destroy the works of the devil" (1 John 3:8). We win because Jesus won. The believer's ability to overcome is from Christ. "Be of good cheer, I have overcome the world" (John 16:33). Swing your individual sword of the Spirit. It is true that Satan came to make war with the saints on earth. He has come down to the earth filled with rage because he knows his time is short (Revelation 12:12). But you can overcome him, by the *blood of the*

Lamb and the word of your testimony (Revelation 12:11). This verse is a real "Satan slapper."

A letter received this morning from our evangelist friend Kevin Shorey confirms this:

> It's time to wage war on the kingdom of darkness! We are engaged in spiritual warfare. The devil has brought us so subtly into a "new age." I am sick of his ways. Let's pull down his strongholds. The only place he belongs is under our feet.
>
> I have friends who say, "You're talking about the devil too much." No one says that we talk about Saddam Hussein too much. His name is all over the news lately as we discuss strategies and plans of how to end his wickedness. So we must talk, plan and discuss strategies on how to end Satan's wickedness.
>
> The best part of it all is that this roaring lion roaming around, seeking whom he may devour, is *toothless!* He is already defeated. He knows his time is running out. Jesus said, "I give *you* authority to overcome *all* the power of the enemy."
>
> Plug into the Power! In this fight it's not how big the dog is in the fight, but how big the fight is in the dog!
>
> So, get in there and fight, flex your knee muscles (kneel and pray), put on the armor of God, and keep holdin' on!

Until the very end Satan will be looking for dominion to establish his evil domain, going to and fro throughout the earth, hoping to inhabit your heart. *Resist the invisible enemy by the invisible power of the Holy Spirit.*

The devil's time is about up. God will cleanse his domain so that Christ and His Bride (the Church—*you*) may dwell safely forever and have access to all realms during His millennial reign.

Jesus, our triumphant Victor, once told Peter: "Satan has asked for you, that he may sift you as wheat. But I have prayed for you, that your faith should not fail" (Luke 22:31–32). What hope and courage it brings to know that He is ever at the right hand of the Father making intercession for us (Hebrews 7:25)! We cannot fail.

11
WHAT TIME IS IT?

W hat time is it?

It is time for "goal setting" and time to get our top priorities straight. *Now* is the accepted time; behold, now is the day of salvation (2 Corinthians 6:2). God gives time to repent but will not withhold judgment forever (Revelation 2:21). "The harvest is past, the summer is ended, and we are not saved!" (Jeremiah 8:20). We are becoming what we shall be.

America is running out of time. Workers are weary, parents frantic, children even haven't a moment to spare, to think. Everyone is busy ice skating frantically in a shrinking circle. I believe that the world is sitting in the front row of the Great Drama. The stage is being set, the props are nearly ready and the Director will soon signal Curtains Up! Jesus will split the eastern skies and come for us.

I was on board a flight from Houston to Tampa, and could not help but overhear a conversation between two scientists. They had just left NASA Space Center and were going to Cape Kennedy for a research project. They discussed how we are exploring space at an unbelievably fast pace, how people are inquisitive as to "what's out there," and many have money saved up to travel into space when the opportunity is available to the general public. Then I was startled to hear one of them assess our burgeoning world—with its pollution, overpopulation—this way: "This planet will be obsolete in ten years."

I pondered, *Will Jesus airlift us in ten more years to the unseen world?* Many Bible scholars believe there is a new dispensation brought in every 2,000 years. We are gaining on a new millennium rapidly. Minutes later, I pulled from the seat pocket in front of me the September 1989 issue of *American Way* magazine. The technology section had an amazing article called "Tokyo in Wonderland." Since Japan's population is crowded into a country smaller than the state of California, surface real estate is no longer available. So, they explained, Japan must go up or down. A 4.2 billion dollar project is under way to build *under the earth*, an underground frontier, housing tunnels, railways.

Upon my return home (this was quite an eye-opening trip!) I found a folder inside *National Geographic* magazine on the topic of the endangered earth, produced by the cartographic division. They opened the article with Genesis 2:9: "And out of the ground made the Lord God to grow every tree that is pleasant to the sight, and good for food; the tree of life also in the midst of the garden" (KJV). Threats of a "global warming trend" burning up the human race and a "nuclear winter" freezing most life-forms do not bode a promise of returning to the splendors of Eden on our own. Rather, a cataclysmic end seems to be in sight.

Before this happens, the natural law of gravity will diminish as the "super natural law" takes over. Believers will rise to meet Christ in the air—no longer held down to this temporary, perishable earth (1 Thessalonians 4:16–17). The things that would hold us back will loose us, let us go. When the trumpet sounds we will be part of the great event. The chains of sickness and limitations will fall as we rise to that eternal place. Daniel saw it coming:

"And many of those who sleep in the dust of the earth shall awake, some to everlasting life, some to shame and everlasting contempt. Those who are wise shall shine like the brightness of the firmament, and those who turn many to righteousness like the stars forever and ever. [Before that time] many shall run to and fro, and knowledge shall increase."

Daniel 12:2–4

According to the Jacksonville *Times Union* newspaper, the average family moves about every five years. Many people change jobs even more frequently. The Federal Aviation Administration has been spending billions of dollars to upgrade their air traffic control systems to accommodate the steady and multiplying increase in air travel. More billions of dollars are needed to replace the eight hundred bridges that are falling apart from overuse. People are running to and fro. People are restless, scurrying here and there, seeking peace and safety and finding none.

People are also pleasure mad. I passed two men at the beach wearing sweatshirts with slogans indicative of the times. Across the chest of one was printed a golden halo and the words, "How much can I get away with and still go to heaven?" The other was a luminous green, printed with an overall pattern of dollar signs and the message, "Please, God, give me a chance to prove to You that I can win the lottery and not become proud."

Joel prophesied that in the last days there would be a revival and we are seeing this. But these are also perilous times, when we need to know that trials will get a little harder. This is not heaven. Clearwater Beach is not heaven. I killed two poisonous snakes in my own yard this week while mowing the grass (a pigmy rattler and a coral snake).

Jeremiah warned us a long time ago that perilous times would come first before Jesus comes. The king said, "I don't want to hear the real truth, that kind of message," and had the prophet dropped into a dry well. Don't panic and throw your mental circuit breaker, but heed the warning concerning the last days so that you are not taken by surprise, unaware of a reality as yet unseen.

Jesus Himself cautioned us to be aware:

"As the lightning comes from the east and flashes to the
west, so also will the coming of the Son of Man be. . . .
Heaven and earth will pass away, but My words will by no
means pass away. But of that day and hour no one knows,
no, not even the angels of heaven, but My Father only. But
as the days of Noah were, so also will the coming of the Son
of Man be. For as in the days before the flood, they were
eating and drinking, marrying and giving in marriage, until
the day that Noah entered the ark. . . . Watch therefore, for
you know neither the day nor the hour in which the Son of
Man is coming."   Matthew 24:27, 35–38; 25:13

They did not believe it would happen because it had never happened
before. They refused to believe in a flood, because they had never
seen rain in history before. When the flood came and took Noah and
only seven believing people away, they realized too late that they
"had missed the boat."

The story of Noah Troyer, an Amish farmer, has always fascinated me. He was born in 1831 in Ohio, then later moved to Iowa.
He labored there as a minister and farmer for many years. During a
serious illness he remained unconscious for a long period of time,
but spoke a repeated warning over and over again.

His wife called friends and family members to witness what he
was saying. She reported that he gave the same message 19 times:

"Just as with Noah before the flood, He is warning me, Noah Troyer, that He is giving America one hundred and twenty years to repent
before it will be destroyed, and it will be too late to repent. People
will be partaking the same sins of fornication, adultery and homosexuality as they were in the days of Noah when God's wrath was full
and he destroyed the earth with a flood. God commanded that they
repent and stop their sinning, and instructed Noah to build the ark. He
is now giving us one hundred and twenty years to get ready before His
wrath will fall on unbelievers, and He will rapture the true believers.
Then, this time he will destroy the earth with fire."

This prediction was made in the year 1878. Add one hundred and twenty years to that, and it would put the coming again of Jesus around the year 1998. Scripture tells us that no man knows the day nor the hour, but it doesn't say he can't know the year. The way things are looking, old Noah Troyer may not be far from wrong.

We are an Easter people living in a Good Friday world. We can rejoice in this miserable, messy world, therefore, because our future is with Him. "Everyone who has this hope in Him purifies himself" (1 John 3:3). Do your homework, get ready. "And always be ready to give a defense to everyone who asks you a reason for the hope that is in you" (1 Peter 3:15). Before his death Paul Billheimer said, "We are members of the 'terminal' or rapture generation."

Jesus spoke a parable, recorded in Matthew 25:1–13. The Kingdom of heaven, He said, is like the ten virgins who went to meet the bridegroom. Five had oil in their lamps and were wise. The foolish did not have adequate oil to last until the arrival of the bridegroom. It is high time for us earthlings to check our oil, to shake ourselves and check the time.

We can become so busy with the mechanics of a ministry that we don't have time to check our own oil. In an emergency, at a moment's notice, what we really are inside will come through for us.

Our daughter April is assistant basketball coach for the women's team at St. Petersburg Junior College. Carl and I were driving home rather late one night after seeing them win an away game. We turned a corner in the north part of St. Petersburg and saw fire and smoke coming from an MGA convertible just like mine. The car had stopped suddenly on the highway ahead of us.

A couple scrambled out. The young man quickly rescued the dalmatian from the back seat and ran to safety. But his wife, so foolish, got out and started rummaging under the front seat for her purse, shielding her eyes from the flames. I hoped that she, too, would run before the gas tank exploded, but—can you believe it? Ignoring our shouts she then went to the trunk of the burning car to remove her jewelry and dresses. What a risk she took! She got what she wanted, but barely escaped with her life and two badly burned hands.

Jesus is coming soon. Events are happening too swiftly to worry about perishables, trifles and things that we cannot take with us. Jesus said that the climax of the ages would happen at such a fast pace that it would be in "one generation." We are getting ready for the greatest event of human history: Jesus is coming back!

God's wrath will be poured out by measure, but His mercy is given without measure. Cash in on His mercy while there is still time to pray. What time is it? It is time to look up, for "your redemption draws near" (Luke 21:28).

Lift up your heads to your coming King, bow before Him and adore Him. Sing! Jesus said, "The hour is coming, and now is, when the dead will hear the voice of the Son of God; and those who hear will live. . . . Those who have done good, to the resurrection of life, and those who have done evil, to the resurrection of condemnation [damnation]" (John 5:25, 29).

The world is in crisis, but God has everything under control. The Iraqi crisis has brought nagging fears about the future. We are headed for the final wrap-up of all things. But isn't it better to know? It is enlightening to me to discern clearly that we are living in the last days!

Jesus forewarned His beloved children that when these things begin, "see that you are not troubled" (Matthew 24:6). In the hour of disturbances, don't be afraid, don't make a fuss over it, see to it that your heart is at rest in your Lord!

God compared the nations to a drop in a bucket. Before Him all nations are as nothing; they are counted by Him as *less* than nothing. He shall blow upon them, and they will wither, and the whirlwind will take them away like stubble (Isaiah 40:15, 17, 24). We need not fear them.

The invisible Kingdom is not meat and drink, but righteousness, peace and joy in the Holy Ghost. Follow after the things that make for peace, and edify one another (Romans 14:17, 19). And let the God of hope fill you will all joy (Romans 15:13).

We are of the fellowship of the unstoppable, the unshakable Kingdom. Our agenda involves another world. We must be

grounded in the Word, not seeking an experience or gloating over
the signs and wonders. We must guard against becoming bloated
with pride while the Holy Spirit is being poured out upon us in these
last days. Rather, we look forward with gleeful anticipation to the
Kingdom to come. We sing with a strange, wild joy. It is our native
land. Folks who have their passports in order, stamped with the seal
of approval in the blood of the Lamb, pray differently from the
fickle masses who only petition Him for selfish wants. Their hearts
are linked to Eternity. They are not anemic in their determination
because they have had a supernatural blood transfusion. Jesus' blood
has cleansed them, making them worthy to be royalty in the Kingdom to come.

People who have a vision of the future there keep their souls'
radar on alert. This generation has been fed a popular diet of religious quick fixes. Our churches have either been overexposed to
supernatural miracles or deadened by social action teaching, and we
are becoming spoiled and spiritually droopy.

I wonder if the people who are not obedient to assemble themselves together in the houses of the Lord to worship Him on His day
each week will be of quality and disposition to be candidates for the
Kingdom at the time of the Rapture. Those who will rule and reign
with God in His authority will be those who have been obedient
here. God rewards faithfulness and obedience.

We are the children of God, heirs of God, joint heirs with Christ.
If we suffer with Him, we shall be glorified together with Him.
(This cancels out a false doctrine of cheap grace.) "The sufferings
of this present time are not worthy to be compared with the glory
that shall be revealed in us" (Romans 8:16–18).

Be transformed by the renewing (renovating) of your mind (Romans 12:2). Renovate your thinking, get ready for what is up ahead.
Be fervent in spirit, rejoicing in the hope of eternal life, which God,
who cannot lie, promised before the world even began (Titus 1:2).

Jesus' final words recorded in the Bible are: "I, Jesus, have sent
My angel to testify to you these things in the churches. I am the

Root and the Offspring of David, the Bright and Morning Star. . . .
Surely I am coming quickly'' (Revelation 22:16, 20).

Our friend Henry Vanderbush is known as ''the barn preacher''
from the Midwest. He came to speak at our church here in Dunedin,
Florida, recently. Tears filled his eyes as he told us: ''Little Billy,
my youngest son, is the joy of my life. My wife always brought him
to the airport to meet my flight whenever I returned from a speaking
tour. The little guy would elbow his way past knees and briefcases
and was always the first in line at the jetway when the plane door
was opened. He would spring, jump and I would catch him. He
would kiss first one cheek then the other, totally unashamed of his
impulsive love for his daddy.

''At the end of one trip, I looked and did not see Billy. Was he
sick? He had never failed to be there to greet me. I asked my wife,
'Where is Billy?' She replied, 'In the game room. I told him your
flight was due. I called him, but Billy has found a new love. He has
learned what a quarter in a video machine will do.' ''

Henry admitted, ''I wept. The change in Billy's love broke my
heart. I could hardly bear it.''

Jesus said, ''I have this against you, that you have left your first
love'' (Revelation 2:4). Many professing Christians, ministries and
even ministers are in the game room, playing religious games. Is
this the church in America today?

But our world today is not business as usual. Jesus is coming for
a remnant, not just warned, but ready. When your walk gets a little
harder, you will become a lot stronger, and He will say, ''Come on
up!'' Suddenly the trumpet will sound. The highest utopia experience, the greatest joy you have ever had in God will intensify. His
powerful joy will come on a little stronger, and you will not be able
to contain it with your natural body. You will be changed, like the
taking off of a powerful jet plane, transported to the place you were
programmed to go before you were born.

The ultimate destiny of the universe, including planet earth, is
being directed from God's golden throne room. He orchestrated
creation, He orchestrated salvation and He will orchestrate Satan's

end. The books of Thessalonians, Corinthians and Revelation chronicle a great deal about the Millennium and the rebirth of the earth, the purged-by-fire earth, the new earth.

We all have questions we would like to ask God. He has promised us a chance to do so during the Millennium. I personally believe that when we come back here during the millennial reign many unfulfilled desires in this life shall be satisfied then. No one would be unequally yoked with unbelievers there, because all there are believers. Any hindrance that prevented a woman from having children in this life would not hinder her there.

There are two sides to the coin, however. There are two definite destinies awaiting us: heaven or hell. The time of judgment will end with the eternal punishment of Satan and sinners. ''They shall be cast into the lake of fire that burns forever.'' (See Revelation 18, 19, 20.)

This past Sunday we were made more keenly aware of Jesus' soon coming, and rejoiced in the ''Blessed Hope.'' Our music director led the chorus while the entire congregation sang that song with great joy and confirmation: ''The Kingdom of God is within me, I know no defeat, only strength and power.'' There was a lull, a creative silence, and we heard the voice of an elderly gentleman from the rear of the church with a word of encouragement. I am so glad they were taping the service, for I feel it was not just for our congregation, but that I should pass it on to you:

''I am the Lord, I have redeemed you by My blood. There is no enemy that is not under My feet this day. You will be enthroned with Me in the heavenlies. You will sit with Me in delightful places. Rejoice in your heart and know that your God is a God who does valiantly for you. There is nothing that He cannot do for you, and surely you shall identify with His total victory. You shall be seated in the realm of faith. Your eyes shall not look upon the darkness of this world. Behold my glory, saith the Lord.

''My faith shall arise within years, I shall energize your tongue and you shall speak a living word to your circumstance, and you shall speak a living flame of fire to your obstacles and they shall melt and be no more! I have called you to be sons and daughters, to sit with Me, to rule with Me; speak and agree with Me this day. I am coming to remind you that we are in covenant and we are delights of hosts, saith God.''

Many people are making predictions. Much of the Bible is devoted to prediction. Nothing God has done for us can compare with all that He has promised to do for us, written in His sure Word of prophecy. This is our heritage of joy!

What time is it? It is time to move into deeper personal relationship with the triune God, to shift our life emphasis from the present to the future, to focus our eyes more and more on the sure tomorrow.

It is almost curtain time! We are rehearsing for kingship . . . practicing for rulership. We are destined for the throne.

12
THE UNREAL WORLD:
THE LAST STOP

O ur exit from this life is our grand entrance up there! It is like everything you have ever seen, and yet like nothing you have ever seen.

"Eye has not seen, nor ear heard, nor have entered into the heart of man the things which God has prepared for those who love Him" (1 Corinthians 2:9). This life here on earth is not it.

I have seen lots of cartoons and jokes about the "end of the world." It is not the end; God is unending and those who serve Him have just begun to live in the forever world to come. We have endless hope, not a hopeless end. I read a bumper sticker yesterday, "Life is hard and then you die." It was probably meant in a funny but "why bother?" attitude. To me it was just the opposite. Life *is* hard, but this only makes the thought of the next world more exciting for the Christian. As Paul said, "If in this life only we have hope . . . we are of all men the most pitiable" (1 Corinthians 15:19). In his book *Facing Death and Life Hereafter*, Billy Graham gives an exciting account of how the Christian faces death—with joy. Earth has no sorrow that heaven cannot heal. How happy we shall be to see Jesus "coming on the clouds of heaven with power and great glory" (Matthew 24:30).

As I mentioned earlier—quoting Mona Johnian—there are three heavens. The third heaven is where God's throne remains intact along with all the glories of the eternal Kingdom. The second heaven is the starry place, where the sun, moon and stars were placed in the firmament at God's command at creation. The first heaven is the atmosphere surrounding the earth, where weather is formed, where birds and airplanes fly. When Jesus comes for us, He will leave the third heaven, His domain, pierce the second, then split the eastern sky of the first heaven near the earth and we shall behold Him in the clouds.

Abraham spent an entire lifetime en route to that city whose builder and maker is God. He endured hardship in this life because he was attached to the future, to the New Jerusalem (Hebrews 11:10). People who know where they are going can continue to persevere for they know what they are expecting at the journey's end! They are thirsty for God and reality found in that country.

We have been promised a mansion eternal in the heavens, not here. I live just four blocks from an incredible housing development on the Gulf Coast. We "pore" folks call it "Conspicuous Consumption Row." One mansion there sold recently for $1.2 million. What size will your mansion be in heaven? I believe it will be large enough to accommodate all those you have been responsible for saving on earth; you will celebrate in your reception hall. Some may need only an efficiency apartment there.

Heaven is not a foggy illusion. We should enjoy "now," but set our sights on "then." Jesus said, "Seek first the kingdom of God and His righteousness, and all these things shall be added to you." Sometimes we get this backward. We seek all the things we want for the now, and plan to receive the Kingdom in the end. It doesn't work that way. How many of our goals are spiritual?

Heaven is not an opiate for the old, to numb their pain and fears "toward the end." It is not just a symbol of better things to come or a metaphor representing our fondest wishes. It is a city with a real foundation.

New York City is loved for her skyscrapers. Boston is known for her history. Moscow is a tourist attraction with her onion-domed architecture and ancient churches. But according to Revelation, in heaven's capitol city, the New Jerusalem, there will not be one shadow, no dark alleys, no crime, no weapons, no hurry . . . and light *everywhere*. The city is surrounded with walls of salvation, bulwarks of peace and safety (Isaiah 26:1). The foundations of the city walls are made of twelve kinds of stones ranging in color from pale lavender, to light green, to dark red, like garnet. They are glorious! (See Revelation 21:9–27.) We have a little foretaste of these foundations in the fact that the breastplate of the priests contained twelve colorful stones (Exodus 28:17–20). A little bit of heaven early on earth.

Revelation talks a lot about books. That makes me happy! Books in heaven! Revelation also speaks about streets of gold on which real people with real feet can walk, talk, worship and commune with each other and the "Lamb of God" who took away our sin when we were in the world below. There are mountains, harpists, musical instruments, singers, rivers, fountains, food, trees, even horses there, and things that cannot be described because of their awesome beauty (2 Corinthians 12:4).

Heaven will be different things to different people. Our temperament will be like His, but our taste and personality will still be ours. I have interviewed several people and asked them the question, "What will heaven mean to you?" Here are some responses.

One elderly man wrote me a letter to thank me for a copy of my last book *Heaven: a Bright and Glorious Place*. He said, "I would like to take all my books to heaven with me, or obtain copies written there. When I get there I want to meet every one of the authors I have read, and get their personal autographs—right after Jesus signs my new Scofield Bible!"

There are no losers in Heaven. I talked with a Christian politician. He plans to keep his integrity here, so that he can "rule and reign with Jesus," during the thousand years of peace here on earth. He understands the Bible to say that he will reign over territories then, as he overcomes here. This is not automatically easy. We will not reign with Him unless we are willing to suffer with Him. To be an overcomer, we must first come over something.

A young man, Peter Brammel, told me that he wants to walk on water on the River of Life in heaven, like Peter in the Bible. There will be no doubt, no fear of water and no danger, for all fear is past.

A mother who lives in Bradenton lost two sons in the Vietnam war. She said she is looking forward to seeing those two boys again, and will watch with great interest the war when Satan will be bound and cast into the lake of fire. Daniel talked of this. There will be no Christian casualties *there*!

A single young man told me, "I have always been introverted in my personality. I was the only Christian in my Jewish family, and 'bucked unbelief' all my life. There, I will belong, have a family that will love me and support me." The young man talked on with great jubilation, "Neither my parents nor my siblings have realized that Jesus was our Messiah, and do not understand when I talk about ruling with Jesus in His coming Kingdom. I can hardly contain myself when I realize that there, I will have true, royal blood Jews for my family! I want to hunt with Nimrod; John the beloved will be my brother, as will Shadrach, Meshack and Abednego; Abraham will be my father, Naomi and Ruth my aunts; I can get together for family occasions with Luke and John; a friendship with Jonathan will develop like the friendship he had on earth with David. What a family I have been adopted into—no, not adopted. We will be *blood* relatives, since Jesus' blood makes us 'one'!"

Carl and I sat with a young man at a baseball game recently. He told me, "Betty, I can hardly wait to get to heaven. I read in the Bible that we will get a new name to fit who we really are, who we have become. The way I understand it, this life is the baseball camp where we try out for the team and are chosen according to our performance. I want that 'white stone' and that new name" (Revelation 2:17).

Sitting nearby was a girl, grinning. She chimed in, "My name is Sue. I want to get rid of it. Too many legal battles; people *sue* for almost anything nowadays." She continued, "In the town where I grew up, my close friend and neighbor was Patty Butts. Her dad was the local town mortician. She has never married but has tried to get rid of that name for a long time!"

I sincerely want a good name both here and there. Some will be named faithful and true.

I have been working with a young woman in Alaska, planning a retreat in February. When her group invited me, I asked them to confirm the date and plans "one more time, please." The director assured me that, yes, she had the nerve to ask a Floridian to come to Alaska in February! She told me that during the "dark-day" season there are many suicides and much depression among women who are trapped by winter. She, herself, moved there from Oklahoma and, though her husband makes good money, she misses the milder climate and sunshine.

When I arrive there they will meet me at the airport with a snowmobile suit, insulated boots and gloves, and I will be driven for two more hours to the camp where the retreat is held.

In the course of our phone conversation, I told her about this chapter and asked her what heaven meant to her. She replied quickly, "I want to travel by 'just wishing' instead of using these four-wheel drive vehicles on snow-packed paths. I want to live in heaven's 'sunny clime' where there's a fruit crop every month of the year."

Kevin Polce works at the All Children's Hospital in Tampa. He has a tender love for the sick, orphaned and handicapped children that he cares for. At Christmas some of the little fellows thought the nurses were angels and the doctors were priests or God. When Kevin bought presents for some of the kids who had no family and received no gifts, they thought he was Santa Claus. Heaven to Kevin will be a place where children are healthy and loved by a family.

When Bernice Kovacs gets to heaven, she is going to have a

homecoming choir performance. All her students who sang in choirs that she directed at colleges on earth can raise their voices in praise in one grand voice! Bernice never had children. These singers over the years have been her kids.

I talked with a woman who is a nun. She told me, "I have been a sister in the Catholic Church since I was very young. I'm married to the Church, but have always wanted babies." She had a vision that in heaven she would be the mother of babies whose earth mothers did not believe in Jesus and did not make it to heaven.

The real estate woman who sold us this little Florida house told me that she has always been "land hungry." She sells a lot of property, but owns just a small lot "the size of a bed sheet." She said, "When I get to heaven, I want lots of land. I've always wanted to own waterfront property." I shared with her some verses from Revelation and that satisfied her. We laughed. Waterfront property here in Florida sells at "so much per foot." There, she will have probably a quarter mile of waterfront along the river of life! That's living it up!

Wouldn't it be rewarding for a schoolteacher here on earth to team teach with Paul? Why not? We have forever, and people who receive Jesus on their deathbeds will need to be discipled after they arrive there.

I talked with an automobile service manager when I had my car repaired this past week. I thought he would tell me that heaven is "no more hydraulic lifts, no more grease on his hands." Instead he wept and told me a tender, personal story: "I'm looking forward to heaven, that place where wrongs are made right. When my young daughter got pregnant out of wedlock, I ran off her boyfriend. The ultrasound revealed that the baby was a boy. This was before I knew Jesus' love and I forced her to have an abortion."

He went on. "Now that I am a Christian, I realize that the innocent baby that never sinned went to heaven. There is nothing incomplete there, for God is completeness. My daughter never did marry, and never had other children. I can hardly wait to get to heaven and see my only grandson. I want to take eternity to make up to him for the love I denied him here on this earth. Until my daughter, my wife and I get there, I am convinced that barren women in this life who are already there will love and teach him, and the angels will be a delight to the little fellow.''

One of the ''runners up'' for the Miss Teen pageant told me that she looks forward to heaven as the place of no misunderstanding. She explained, ''Being pretty is a definite disadvantage. Many people mistake my erect carriage as haughty pride, my confidence as superiority and my friendliness as flirting. My outgoing personality has gotten me into some jams.'' (Perhaps you, the reader, have always wanted to be beautiful. Go to that place where looks are not a qualification for entrance.)

Her friend sitting nearby added, ''Golden streets! That's what I want to see, those golden streets. I grew up in Arkansas in the country and have been poor all my life. We lived down a remote, gravel road. On Saturday night Dad would wash the car so it would be clean for Sunday school. By the time we got to the highway, it was dusty and dirty again.

''My brothers and I still have gravel in our elbows from sliding on our bikes on that rutty road. During the hot summer it was dusty. Then when the rain came we got, not just rain, but gully washers, and the ruts were awful. One rather wealthy man had the money and put asphalt on the section of road in front of his big house. We kids thought it was heaven to ride our bikes on that asphalt strip of road. Yes, I want to ride a bike on a smooth, golden street!''

One high school athlete said he loves hurdles and relay races at field-and-track days, but he is never fast enough to place in the competition. ''There I'll be swift. The Bible tells me I'll be changed in a twinkling of an eye.''

I am amazed that since starting this book, I seem to have come across illustrations I need at exactly the time I am writing on that particular subject. I was switching TV channels one day and caught an interview. The young woman in the wheelchair was a victim of birth defects. She had no fingers or toes. She had a jolly sense of humor, however, and stated confidently that ''in heaven, I'll have long, slender fingers and play a harp. David, the psalmist, will instruct me there.''

For Jodi Stuart heaven will be "riding a white horse." I met her this spring when I spoke at a Methodist day of prayer on the East Coast. As I left the conference headed toward the airport, a young couple with a tiny baby intercepted me at the door.

The young husband held the baby while his wife approached me. She told me that she had suffered cardiac arrest during the Caesarean section performed just three weeks before. She said, "The doctors told me that during the crisis I was dead—gone for about four minutes, according to my heart monitor.

"Now I have always loved horses, but been terrified of them. I have hated myself that I prevented myself from ever experiencing a horseback ride because of this awful fear.

"During my out-of-body experience, I stood on a bluff, a plateau or mesa, at a high altitude overlooking an immense meadow of lush grass. It was waving in the breeze—velvet grass unlike anything natural. In that meadow were thousands of white horses. They were not grazing slowly, but nibbling on the grass with a spirit of anticipation; not lined up in any order or garrison, but alert and ready for some event. I strangely knew that one of those horses was *mine!* I have talked to so many people about this vision or whatever, and everyone just tells me it was because I had no oxygen to my brain, or because of drugs. I know it is much more. Those horses were not imaginary, but alive, and I had been personally chosen to ride one of them.

"Betty, I did not know you were coming to our city until a few minutes ago when I spotted the ad announcing the prayer conference where you would tell about your glimpse of eternity. I hurried, hoping to see you before you left town. I received Jesus as my Savior when I was a little girl in vacation Bible school, but haven't been going to church, and don't have a minister. Can you tell me what those horses meant?''

She looked fearful that I, too, would think she had brain damage, though it was plain to see that she was a sharp young woman. I got so excited, I literally trembled while listening to her talk. It is so wonderful to tell someone something who hasn't heard everything! She was so thirsty to hear good news. I sat in the front seat of their car, opened the Bible and began reading to her from Revelation:

> And I heard, as it were, the voice of a great multitude, as the sound of many waters and as the sound of mighty thunderings, saying, "Alleluia! For the Lord God Omnipotent reigns!" . . . Then I saw heaven opened, and behold, a white horse. And He who sat on him was called Faithful and True, and in righteousness He judges and makes war. His eyes were like a flame of fire, and on His head were many crowns. . . . And His name is called The Word of God. And the armies in heaven, clothed in fine linen, white and clean, *followed Him on white horses.*
>
> Revelation 19:6, 11–14

Elsie Dixon from Cincinnati, whose family shared this story with me, saw Him coming from that heavenly city. On August 21, 1988, she lay in a hospital bed dying with cancer. Her seven children and some of their spouses had gathered to help her die.

Years earlier, Elsie's marriage had ended in grief. Her husband, Otis, a minister, had been a godly man, a fine craftsman of evangelism. But the very listening quality that made him an exceptional counselor became his trap. The trap snapped shut, locking him into unfaithfulness. When he went down the crash was loud. It shook the community and his family was nearly destroyed. He had been strict about things that were petty compared to his own wrong. The pieces of his life were strewn in disorder.

One of his sons explained, "Dad cut himself off and left the scene. We could have forgiven him if he had but asked. Instead he ran away and went to Missouri where he attended a little church. Eventually God's mercy restored his soul, but his testimony and integrity had diminished. He preached only occasionally to a few in a few churches. When we learned he had been restored in his relationship to God, we continued to pray that he would return and be reconciled to our family and our mother. Sadly enough, before this happened he died very suddenly and unexpectedly of a massive heart attack. Mother's heart seemed broken.''

Now Elsie lay dying. With her last breath, she asked that there not be any machines, so she could die in dignity. "If I die, I want nothing holding me back from my heavenly home." Then looking around the bed, seeing the faces of some of her children with wounded spirits who had drifted from the Lord, she spoke plainly, "If you ever want to see me again after tonight, you will have to return to Him, and allow God to rule your lives."

The cancer had severed her vertebrae and she had not been able to lie on her back, but the nurse turned her on her back so she could see all of her family clearly. The quiet of the room spoke "helpless." The nurse checked her. Her vital organs had "shut down."

One son Ken grieved that his mother, Elsie, would not live long enough to enjoy her first great-grandchild. She had grieved so when another grandchild, Kerri, had been hit and killed at a school crossing.

Suddenly Elsie was staring up at the ceiling. She pointed a finger and exclaimed, "I can see through the ceiling! Oh! The full moon is so close, so round and so bright, getting closer to me. It is gorgeous!" How did she know? Later on that night of August 21 after dark there would be a full moon, but it was not visible at that time of day. She was transcending earth through time and space!

She continued to describe her journey: "I'm in the sky! Now I'm going through heaven's gates! I am! I really am! It is so beautiful! It is *so* bright!" Then, with a half-whispered tenderness, she sobbed, "I see Dad. I see Otis. He made it. His loving arms are reaching for me. He really is coming toward *me!*"

The lid of hate and resentment that had imprisoned the family feelings for so long, blew off. Shouts exploded from throats as each cried out in his or her own way. Those who had never doubted where their father had gone, cried out in longing to see him again. For others, assurance of their dad's salvation being restored created a tearful reaction.

During those moments, the silent wonder of the good and happy "growing up years" surfaced again.

Elsie's enjoyment of her discovery lasted for a long time. She lay there telling, reporting, explaining in great detail with gleeful exuberance. She exclaimed, "I see Kerri! I see my own dear mom and dad." She went on to describe the sights and sounds, quoted the songs, then joined the singing. Her walk through the new world, unseen to her family, can only be compared to a child who has many wonderful presents to open on Christmas morning. Her chronicle of indescribable surroundings was a treasure presenting itself to her.

Then suddenly she became very still. Slowly raising her hands, she covered her eyes and shouted loudly, "Praise be to God!" This was not the mother that the family had known! It was such a contrast to her quiet personality, and the silent way she had always been known to worship. When her hands came down, her face was aglow. She had seen Jesus, the Gift of gifts. She told her family, "I'm talking to Jesus. He is healing me!"

Whispering, she informed them, "It seems that I shall be coming back. I am above you . . . flying toward you. Angel escorts are bringing me back—beautiful angels!" She sighed and addressed her daughter Shirley: "You are not here with me."

She opened her eyes, smiled and remarked with chagrin, "Well, here I am. I'm back." She got up and said, "Don't hold me down. I am healed!" She had tremendous strength that she had retained from her heavenly journey. She had supernatural joy for four hours.

I know the members of this family and they are not starry-eyed folks who are still intoxicated by the heady presence of the Holy Spirit. The family was firmly planted in Pentecost and the truth that miracles do happen, but they were not standing by this bedside open-armed, ready to embrace every new experience as being sealed by that same Spirit. The years of experience had made them wise enough to know that even good, honest people, without even realizing it, can want a thing so badly that they see or hear what they want to see or hear, when it really isn't there.

The events of that night, however, were too precious for them to allow even a shadow of doubt to fall. Tingling with the gift their mother had given them, they set about dealing with its meaning for them.

Elsie continued to discuss the things she had seen in the invisible (to them) world. They were satisfied that she knew not only where she was and what was happening to her, but also where she had been and with whom she had been! She fully realized that she had moved back and forth between two realms, both equally real! Her face retained the radiance for four hours.

Then she said, "No more questions."

At 1:15 A.M. she looked up, smiled and said, "Goodbye."

What was the purpose of this experience? Why did Elsie come back? If it had to do with healing, then who was healed? Jesus heals all kinds of diseases, infirmities and bitternesses against those who disappoint us. How many of these were healed that night? What do we know about the length of God's arm of mercy?

The family came to the hospital to help Elsie die. She came back to help them live! She left us an indelible message: There is an invisible world around us that is more real than the one we see!